D1559834

Lake of the Woods
Yesterday and Today

by Duane R. Lund, Ph. D.

Printed by
Nordell Graphic Communications, Inc.
Staples, Minnesota 56479

Distributed by
Adventure Publications, Inc.
P.O. Box 269
Cambridge, Minnesota 55008

ISBN 0-934860-03-3

TABLE OF CONTENTS

8th Printing
April 1993

7th Printing
November 1988

6th Printing
March 1984

5th Printing
May 1980

4th Printing
May 1978

3rd Printing
May 1977

2nd Printing
January 1976

Copyright © 1975 by
Dr. Duane R. Lund
Staples, Minnesota 56479

Printed in the United States of America

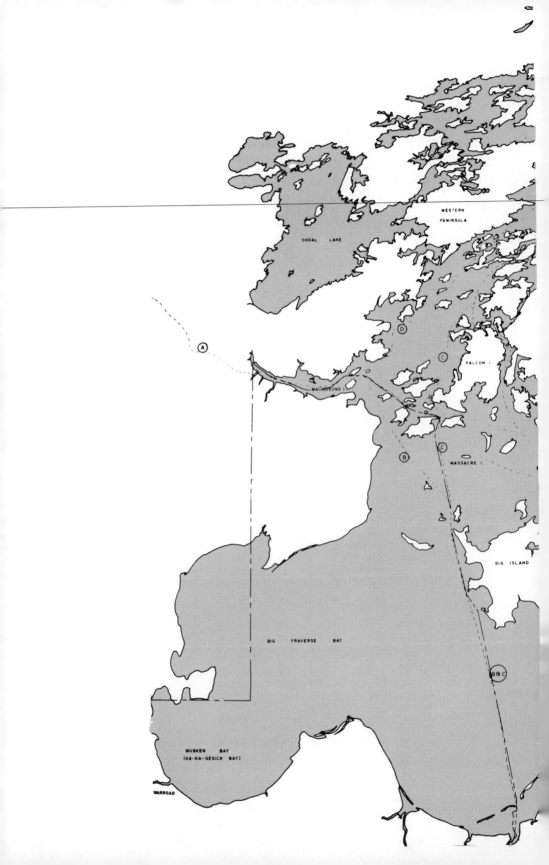

WESTERN
PENINSULA

SHOAL   LAKE

Ⓓ

Ⓐ

Ⓓ

Ⓒ

FALCON I

MAGNUSONS I.

Ⓒ

Ⓑ

Ⓒ

MASSACRE I.

BIG   ISLAND

BIG   TRAVERSE   BAY

ⒷⒷ Ⓒ

MUSKEG   BAY
(KA-KA-GESICK   BAY)

WARROAD

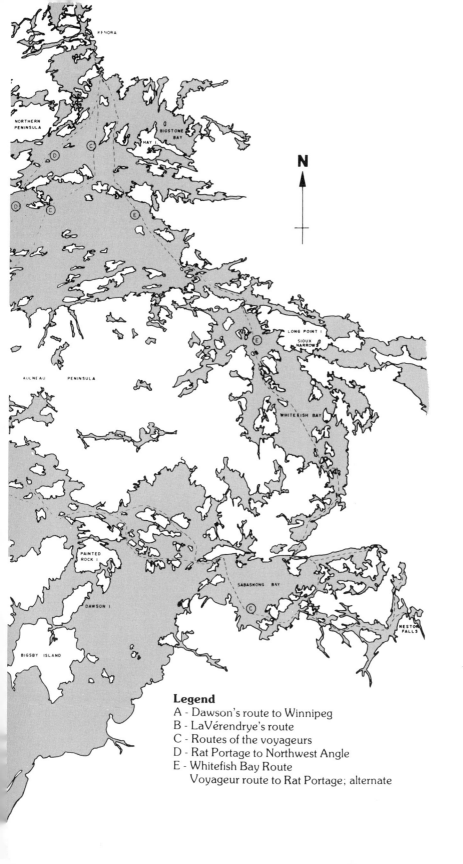

N

Legend
A - Dawson's route to Winnipeg
B - LaVérendrye's route
C - Routes of the voyageurs
D - Rat Portage to Northwest Angle
E - Whitefish Bay Route
    Voyageur route to Rat Portage; alternate

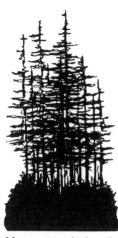

CHAPTER I
The Age of Discovery and Exploration

PERSPECTIVE

The year is 1688.

George Washington has not yet been born. Daniel Boone will not be exploring the eastern wilderness for nearly 100 years. More than a century will pass before Zebulon Pike and Henry Schoolcraft will come to Minnesota in search of the source of the Mississippi. It will be over one hundred and fifteen years before Lewis and Clark are commissioned to explore the west. In France, Louis XIV is on the throne. In England, Oliver Cromwell is out and royalty has been restored in the person of William of Orange. Peter the Great rules Russia. And Napoleon will not meet his "Waterloo" until one hundred and twenty-seven years into the future.

The year is 1688.

A twenty-year-old French lad, Jacques De Noyon, and his Indian companions guide their canoes around the last bend in the Rainy River. De Noyon becomes the first white man to see one of the most beautiful and exciting bodies of water in all the world - *The Lake of the Woods.*

As the young explorer viewed the vast expanse of water - which reached to the very skies on the western horizon - he must have thought he had found a great inland sea, or perhaps that he had discovered the long-sought-route to the Pacific Ocean itself. However, as De Noyon continued his explorations, he found that it was neither the Pacific nor even a body of water the size of Lake Superior. Yet, it was one of the largest lakes he had encountered. As he wandered north through the countless passageways and in and out among the islands he must have wondered if the maze would ever end. Appropriately he named it "Lac Aux Isles" (Lake of the Isles).

What was De Noyon doing in the middle of the continent three centuries ago? Primarily, he was interested in furs. Even at that early date, the merchants of Montreal and other eastern settlements were concerned about the depletion of fur-bearing animals along the eastern waterways and the competition to the north from the Hudson's Bay Company. The young explorer had been headquartered in the Rainy Lake area and had heard from friendly Indians of the great sea not far to the west.

THE LAKE'S FIRST RESIDENTS

Although we have a good account of the exciting history of Lake of the Woods since its discovery in 1688, virtually nothing is known for certain of the years before the white man's coming when it was the exclusive domain of the Indians. It is interesting how we are inclined to mark the beginning of all things with their discovery by white man. We know, of course, that it was actually thousands of years before Europeans came to North America when the first man set eyes on our lake. To put this in its proper perspective, it is very probable that the span of time represented by white man's association with this area is less than 5% of human history on the lake. Archeologists tell us that several thousands of years ago, the Lake of the Woods was part of Lake Agassiz, that inland sea which was created by the melting of the Pliestocene Glacier. Lake of the Woods, Lake Winnipeg, and Lake Manitoba are the larger remnants of this lake. The ancient shoreline of Lake Agassiz can still be traced. One such shore has been called Campbell Beach and stretches through central Lake of the Woods and Roseau Counties. This was at one time the northern boundary of the inhabited world, because across Lake Agassiz lay only glaciers. On this ancient shoreline lived a people. Their burial mounds contain remnants of pottery, shell ornaments, and stone weapons and tools, but in addition artifacts of ivory have also been discovered - indicating that these early inhabitants were contemporary with the wooly mammoth, and used their tusks as material for spears, weapons, and simple tools. These early hunters brought down such game as the giant bison with their finely made, leaf-shaped spears. A hand-worked piece of antler, discovered near Morson, Ontario, is the earliest dated specimen found thus far in the area - radiocarbon tests indicate that it may be 8,000 years old.[1] By this standard, De Noyon was a "Johnny-come-lately" on the Lake of the Woods scene!

Copper tools and weapons found in the Lake area have been dated at 2000 B.C. This would make them the earliest metal items fabricated by the native people of either North or South America. Copper artifacts were excavated by Dr. Walter Kenyon at Pither's Point (International Falls) in 1959 - including a copper gaff. Other copper items of this early period were found at Houska's Point (Ranier).

It was also about 2000 B.C. that the approximate present shoreline of Lake of the Woods was established. Water levels were raised several feet,[2] of course, by the construction of the dams at the north end of the Lake early in this century.

Hundreds of burial mounds along both sides of the Rainy River tell the story of a much later people, the "Laurel Culture". One such mound, located at the confluence of the Big Fork and Rainy Rivers is about 40 feet high and is called the Grand Mound. This is the largest remaining burial mound in the upper Mississippi region. It has never been excavated. Some of the Skeletal remains from the Laurel period were of a race larger and heavier than modern-day Indian. The bones were buried in bundles, indicating that the bodies had originally been placed on scaffolds or in shallow graves and allowed to decompose. Shell ornaments were found which have been determined to have come from either the Gulf of Mexico or the Pacific.

Archeologists suspect that mound building was learned from the Hopewell Indians of southern Minnesota.

The Laurel people are also credited with bringing the bow and arrow to the area.

Somewhere around 1000 A.D., a new people arrived establishing the Blackduck Culture. Whether they pushed the Laurel people out or assimilated them, is not known, - perhaps some of each. These people dominated the Lake of the Woods and Rainy Lake area until the 1700's. The Blackduck people buried their dead in pits, and then built mounds over the remains. Two such burial mounds dated 1200 A.D. are located at the mouth of the Rainy River on the old Hungry Hall Reserve. The contents of these two mounds are among the most spectacular found in central North America. They included seven skulls, - modeled and decorated with paint, as well as a variety of

---

[1]*It should be noted that the validity of the radio carbon technique of measuring time beyond 6 000 years is now questioned by some.*
[2]*About nine feet.*

Prehistoric Mound, at Mound Park, Laurel Minn. Height 28 ft. Width 115 ft. One of the largest Mounds found built by the Prehistoric Race, called "Mound Builders."

complete vessels, catlinite[1] and steatite[2] tubes, shell gorgets[3] bead jewelry made from shells, bones, and antlers, etc.

The rock paintings found on Lake of the Woods and along other water passageways in Ontario are thought to come from the Blackduck Culture. These ancient examples of Indian art are to be found at several locations around the lake, including (1) a point near Dead Man's portage between Shoal Lake and Lake of the Woods, (2) between Painted Rock Island and Split Rock Island near the west entrance to Sabaskong Bay, and (3) in Blindfold Lake. The durability of the paints used has mystified many; they are thought to have been made from berry juice, spruce gum, fish oils or tallow, and certain minerals. It has been said that "the paint used by the Indians never dies".

The Lake of the Woods must have had a great attraction for mankind down through the centuries; it had so much to offer. First, it was difficult to move north, south, east, or west in this central part of North America without using the waters of this sprawling lake for transportation. Indians on the move could come onto the Lake from the east and south by Rainy River, from the plains of the south and west by the Warroad River, and it was joined to Hudson Bay and the vast northland (including what is now western Canada) by the Winnipeg River. The waters of the lake flow north and empty into the Winnipeg River through three shoots or falls.

The Lake of the Woods had so much to offer its people for survival. The lake itself, with its thousands of miles of irregular shoreline, provided ideal spawning grounds for the propagation of all kinds of fish. Sheltered bays yielded thousands of acres of wild rice. The forests were filled with game and fur-bearing animals of all kinds which provided food and clothing. Ducks, geese, and grouse were in abundance. Birch

---

[1] Red clay or pipestone from which the Indians made pipes for smoking.
[2] Green-gray or brown soap stone from which pipes were made.
[3] Neck ornaments.

forests provided material for canoes and shelter from the elements. Rock, from which tools and weapons could be made, was everywhere. Best of all, transportation was easy. Apart from Big Traverse, the waterways were sheltered by high bluffs and tall forests. Such hazards as waterfalls and rapids were almost nonexistent.

But it may have been too ideal. During the first century of white man's contact with the area, there seemed to be an almost continuous struggle for possession of the lake between the woodland Indians (the Cree and Ojibway) and the Indians of the plains (the Sioux). There is every reason to believe that tribal wars characterized the history of Lake of the Woods for centuries prior to the arrival of the French explorers. As the white man pushed the Indians inland from the east coast, the eastern Indians, now armed with guns, in turn pushed rival tribes still farther west. When the Frenchmen

from The International Commission Final Report, 1917

His ancestors were among the first residents of the Lake of the Woods.

first came to this area, some called it Lac aux Assiniboines - after a tribe they found here; others called it Lac aux Christineaux (Crees) - after another tribe of the area. During the years of discovery and exploration, the Chippewa (Ojibway) moved in from the Sault Ste. Marie area. They made peace with the Crees and Monsonis who were already on the Lake when the first white man came but were at constant war the Sioux, who were to the south and west of the lake. Eventually (by 1800) the Assiniboines had moved to Lake Winnipeg and then further west to the Canadian plains and foothills. The Crees also had moved northward into Manitoba. The Sioux never were successful in their effort to capture the area; this left control of the Lake of the Woods pretty much in the hands of the Chippewa (Ojibway) by 1800.

It isn't hard to picture the lake as it might have been prior to De Noyon's discovery. We can imagine Indian villages along the shores and on the larger islands. Although the Indians were a wandering people, we know that some village sites were in use hundreds of years. It is thrilling to think of scores of birchbark canoes gliding over clear waters with towering pine, cedar, spruce, aspen, and birch as background. Late summer blueberry picking and September wild rice harvests must have been spectacular tribal happenings. Romanticists could write many a story of the courtship of the Indian maiden by the young brave in an evening setting with the full moon rising over a rocky cliff and the beams filtering through the pines to the waters below, with the haunting cries of a loon for musical background.

Even when we think more realistically of the fight for survival against the long, cold winters with ice as much as three feet thick and snow drifts waist deep, we can't help

Sioux teepees and Chippewa lodge.   Courtesy Minnesota Historical Society

but feel the Indians' chances here were at least better than average. The wilderness was hard, the wilderness was cruel; but the odds for survival in the Lake of the Woods area were surely better than in most parts of the North.

Interestingly enough, the Indians considered the Lake of the Woods as four separate lakes. As was their custom, they gave each lake a name descriptive of the area: "Pequona" which means waters of the sandhills, describes the southern end of the lake including Buffalo Bay, Muskeg Bay,[1] and Big Traverse. "Whitefish" was the

---

[1] *Muskeg Bay has been renamed for Chief Ka-Ka-Gesik, a lifelong resident of Warroad, Minnesota, who was considerably more than 100 years old when he died.*

name given the eastern arm, "Clearwater" describes the western arm, and "Lake of the Woods" applied to the northern portion. These names appear in the records of the Hudson's Bay Company as late as 1872.

FORT ST. CHARLES . . PIERRE LA VERENDRYE . . FATHER ALNEAU . . MASSACRE ISLAND

No wilderness or western saga - ficticious or real - has more drama, tragedy, heroism, adventure, or color than this chapter of Lake of the Woods history. And few are better documented. We are especially indebted to the disciplined record keeping of our explorer hero, Pierre Gautherier De La Verendrye. The records of the Church of France and the Order of the Jesuits bear witness to the authenticity of La Verendrye's journals. Letters from Father Jean Pierre Alneau (a missionary hero of the days of exploration) to his mother and sister in France, which were kept in the family for generations,[1] also collaborate the explorer's diaries.

Since the exploration takes place so early in the history of North America, it is somewhat surprising that although La Verendrye is often called a "French explorer", he was actually born on this continent - at Three Rivers, Quebec, in 1685. His father was governor of that settlement, and his mother was the daughter of a former

Courtesy Minnesota Historical Society

Maple Syrup Camp

Governor, Pierre Boucher. Three Rivers was the "launching pad" for many of the explorations of that century, so it is quite natural that a boy raised in this heroic atmosphere would turn his eyes to the still unknown areas of the West.

---

[1] In 1899, a descendant of the Alneau family gave a packet of letters [already 150 years old] to three Jesuit Priests who had come to Vendre, France in that year. The packet had been passed down from generation to generation and included not only Father Alneau's letters to his family and fellow priests but also letters from Jesuits in North American to the martyr's mother after his death.

It was from Three Rivers that missionaries Breboeuf, Lalemant, Le Jeune, and Daniel began their journey which ended in martyrdom at the hands of the Mohawks.

It was from Three Rivers that Joliet and Marquette launched their explorations to the Great Lakes and Minnesota.

It was from Three Rivers that La Salle ventured toward Illinois.

It was from Three Rivers that the story came of young Radisson, a founder of the Hudson's Bay Company, who was carried away by the Iroquois at the age of sixteen, escaped, was recaptured, and was saved from a death of burning at the stake by an old Indian woman.

And it was from Three Rivers that De Noyon set forth to build a fort on Rainy River and make his mark in history as the first white man to see the Lake of the Woods.

For every explorer or priest associated with this Quebec village whose name is remembered in our history books, there were no doubt several others now long

Canoe Building, Oak Point, 1901

forgotten. Young La Vérendrye must have known many of these men and heard first-hand their tales of success and failure, glory and hardship. As son of the governor, he was in a privileged position.

In an age when travel was often a hardship and always time consuming, La Vérendrye saw a lot of the world. He joined the army at the age of twelve! He fought the British in Boston and the men of the Duke of Marlborough in Flanders. He suffered nine wounds and was left for dead on that foreign battlefield. On his return to Canada he was named Commander of a small trading post on the St. Maurice River. By 1729 he had earned a more responsible post on Lake Nipigon (Ontario). Not far from Nipigon was Fort Kaministikwia (the actual Fort William), beyond which not much of the West was known.

No doubt the Indians and trappers who came to the fort on Lake Nipigon found an eager listener in its commandant. For centuries, the ultimate goal of most European explorers had been to find a shorter way to the Orient. Since the first colonists set foot on North America, each explorer hoped that he would be the one to find the legendary "Northwest Passage" to the Pacific. La Vérendrye probably questioned everyone about the routes west. It is not difficult, therefore, to imagine his excitement when an Indian, "Auchagah" by name, told him that he had traveled to Lake of the Woods and still farther west, and talked of an even larger body of water. La Vérendrye was so excited he recorded in his diary that on three successive nights he dreamed that he had discovered "the great sea of the west". Other Indians confirmed the story of a "great river which could be followed west to a great sea". We know that La Vérendrye summarized his notes in a report which he sent, along with a map sketched by Auchagah on birchbark, to Beauharnois, the Governor of Canada. We even know the name of the messenger. He was Father de Gonar, a missionary who was returning east after attempted to work with the Sioux in the Mississippi region.

In 1730, La Vérendrye responded to an invitation from Governor Beauharnois to meet with him and the colony's engineer, Chauusegros de Lery, in Quebec. Following this conference, a report was prepared for the Minister of Colonies in France and dispatched along with an encouraging recommendation from the Colonial authorities. It was fortunate for La Vérendrye that communications were slow. By the time the discouraging reply arrived, La Verendrye had persuaded the Governor to authorize him to (1) solicit financial support from Montreal merchants, (2) construct three forts at Rainy Lake, Lake of the Woods, and Lake Winnipeg, and (3) trade for furs with the Indians as partial compensation for his explorations. La Vérendrye was already on his way when the reply came from Paris saying that it would allocate no funds for the endeavor.

La Vérendrye probably had much less difficulty enlisting the support of the Montreal merchants than the French government. They were starting to feel the competition of the British as a result of Indians traveling north to Hudson Bay with their furs. It is also likely that even in this early date the animals were being "trapped out" along the eastern waterways.

The La Vérendrye party left Montreal June 5, 1731. Although he had a crew of fifty men, it was quite a family affair. Included were three of La Vérendrye's sons: Jean Baptiste, Pierre, and Francois, and a nephew, Christophe Dufrost de La Jemeraye. They passed through Lachine and traveled down the Ottawa. When they reached Fort Machilimackinac, they picked up a Jesuit missionary who was familiar with the country, Father Mesaiger; this completed the authorized contingent of fifty men. One cannot overstate the contributions of men of God such as these in the exploration and eventual settlement of the Americas.

The next stop was Kaministikwia (Fort William); in twelve weeks they had traveled a thousand miles. On August 6th they arrived at the Grand Portage, - after traveling westward along the north shore of Lake Superior. "Grand Portage" meant a rugged nine mile climb up a rise of 650 feet from Lake Superior to the Pigeon River. Because of the lateness of the season and the rugged country ahead, most of the men opposed going farther. After serious deliberation, La Vérendrye agreed to return to Fort Kaministikwia on Lake Superior with the bulk of his men. A smaller group - perhaps volunteers - agreed to go on under the leadership of the nephew, La Jemeraye. Jean Baptiste, the oldest son, accompanied the smaller group. This advance contingent was able to reach Rainy Lake without incident and built a fort at the outlet of Rainy Lake before winter set in. It is believed that the structure was located on Pither's Point at the source of the Rainy River. The fort was named Fort St. Pierre, in honor of Pierre La Vérendrye.

In the spring of 1732, La Jemeraye returned to his uncle with a glowing report and canoes filled with furs. It is easy to imagine the ecstacy which must have filled the anxious heart of La Vérendrye after the long winter of waiting. Although the reunion at Grand Portage took place on May 29, the party did not arrive at Fort St. Pierre until July 14. A smaller party, meanwhile, had headed east after the reunion, bringing the canoes of furs back to Montreal to gladden the hearts of the merchant sponsors of the expedition. We are told that "a large gathering of Indians" met La Vérendrye upon his arrival at the Rainy River Fort (St. Pierre). After considerable speechmaking and the exchange of gifts, the adventurers, accompanied by about fifty Indian canoes, continued westward up the Rainy River to the Lake of the Woods. It must have been quite a spectacle.

Although trappers, traders, and even missionaries no doubt reached Lake of the Woods between the time of its discovery by De Noyon (1688) and the arrival of the La Vérendrye party (1732), few such visits are recorded.

We do know, however, that in 1717, the trader De la Noue, built a post at the mouth of the Kaministikwia River and, following the footsteps of De Noyon, penetrated to Rainy Lake, where he also established a fort.

Five years later the explorer Pachot made the first known chart of the Pigeon River and followed this more southerly water route west to the Lake of the Woods. This southerly route then became the better known and most favored route followed by subsequent travelers.

The reconstructed Fort St. Charles   Courtesy Minnesota Historical Society

After crossing Big Traverse the La Vérendrye party traveled until they came to the inlet of the Northwest Angle. Apparently Divine guidance was sought for the location of the Fort, because we are told it was Father Measiger who advised this particular site. The site was then mainland. Changing water levels caused by the construction of the dams at Kenora made it an island. The structure was built at the mouth of the inlet. Many years later, after the Fort had disappeared in decay, the island was called "Magnusons Island", a name which continues to this day. When the Fort was completed, it was called "Fort St. Charles", perhaps in honor of the priest and Marquis Charles de Beauharnois, the Governor of Canada.

Two descriptions of the Fort are available to us. The Governor of Canada, in a report to the French Colonial Minister in Paris, wrote concerning La Vérendrye:

"He has constructed another Fort west on Lake of the Woods, distant 60 leagues from Tecamamiouen [Rainy Lake]. The interior of this Fort measures 100 feet. It has four bastions. There is a house for the missionary, a church and another house for the commandant, four main buildings with chimneys, a powder magazine, and a storehouse. There are also two gates on opposite sides and a watch tower, and the stakes are in a double row and 15 feet out of the ground."

Father Alneau, the successor to Father Measiger, gave this description in one of his letters dated 1736:

"It consisted of an enclosure made with four rows of posts 12 to 15 feet high in the form of an oblong square within which are several rough cabins constructed of logs and clay and covered with bark."

Apparently the choice of the location was a good one, and the construction although not imposing, must have been well done. There is no record of any attack. We do know, however, that on several occasions the men were worried about attacks and the activities of war parties on the lake, but the structure and those who occupied it were sufficiently impressive to discourage any actual confrontation. Although the Crees and Assiniboines were friendly, the Sioux were a perpetual threat. The Chippewa (Ojibway) who came about that time were traditional enemies of the Sioux and quickly allied themselves with the French.

We know from La Vérendrye's journals that hunting and fishing were excellent in the area and wild rice was abundant. La Vérendrye brought seeds, with him and a garden was planted at the Fort. So far as we know, the first vegetables[1] harvested in the West were at Fort St. Charles.

Jean Baptiste, the eldest son, had not accompanied the group that established the Fort, but had continued east with the canoes (filled with furs) which had met La Vérendrye at Grand Portage in the spring. However, in November of 1732 he joined his father at the Fort just in time for the freeze up and the first long winter at the outpost.

In the spring of 1733, La Jemeraye (appointed second in command by his uncle) led a crew back east to report on the success of the mission. He took with him maps of their discoveries and furs collected over the winter. Father Measiger had been in ill health for some time and chose to return east with the party.

The summer of 1733 passed without incident. As cold weather came on, La Vérendrye dispatched a small party of men to set up a winter camp near a river "where fishing was plentiful". This was probably Grassy River, which enter the lake near Morson (Ontario).

La Vérendrye also recorded a fall expedition (probably to Whitefish Bay) which resulted in a huge catch including 4000 whitefish and numerous trout and sturgeon.

Winter made travel difficult, yet we know there was considerable movement of men in spite of the hardships. There was, of course, only one way to travel in winter - on foot. The only aid was snowshoes. La Vérendrye records in his journal of December 28th, that two Indians visited the encampment from Fort. St. Pierre (at Rainy Lake). They brought disturbing news that "300 Monsonis were singing the song of war". The

[1]*Most sources say corn and peas; others say wheat.*

Sioux had killed four Crees and their women were crying for revenge and accusing the men of cowardice. A few days later another messenger arrived underscoring the urgency of the situation and asking that La Vérendrye come to Fort St. Pierre in person - immediately. It is interesting and important to note that on December 30 (unrelated to the difficulties at Fort St. Pierre) a large band of Assiniboines and Crees arrived from the Lake Winnipeg area. They had heard about the French outpost and sought an alliance with the whites. After the customary speeches and exchanging of gifts, La Vérendrye felt assured that he had developed bonds of freindship which would be helpful to him as he explored further west. We know that the French in general were well received by the Indians, and La Vérendrye was no exception. He was both liked and respected by the friendly Indian tribes.

After receiving the second expression of concern, La Vérendrye, accompanied by his eldest son and a crew of eight men, left for the Rainy Lake fortification. This was the coldest time of the year, yet they made the journey in nine days. Anyone who has traveled the Lake of the Woods in winter has to marvel at the sheer stamina and courage of the men of that time.

Fort St. Pierre had been constructed in an area which supported many Indian villages, and it soon became a gathering place for not only Indians but traders and missionaries. We don't know how many Indians were in the area at the time of La Vérendrye's visit, but a few years later, a missionary wrote, "Generally from two to five thousand Indians in immediate vicinity of the company's fort; and during a part of the year their numbers may be estimated at not less than 2000. Rainy Lake is one of the principal places in the country for holding the Great Medicine feasts".

The Indians listened to La Vérendrye and agreed to postpone their proposed war expedition until spring, providing he would permit his oldest son, Jean Baptiste, to travel with them. Reluctantly, **La Vérendrye** gave his word and began the difficult journey back. He returned to Fort St. Charles physically weakened and suffering from a re-opening of the wounds he had received in France.

In early March - before the ice went out - La Vérendrye sent two of his men on a scouting expedition to Lake Winnipeg. Their mission was to choose a site for the erection of the third fort (as was specified in La Vérendrye's commission).

With spring break-up the Indians from the Rainy Lake area arrived at Fort St. Charles with a huge war party, expecting La Vérendrye to make good his promise to lend them his son to travel with them as they sought revenge on the Sioux. It must have been a traumatic experience for the father. He wrote in his journal:

> *"How can I place my eldest son in the hands of these barbarians? Who knows that my son will ever return or that he will not be made prisoner by the Mascoutans Paunes, the sworn enemies of the Crees and Monsonis, who want me to let him go. On the other hand, if I refuse to let him go, I have reason to fear they will charge me with cowardice and come to the conclusion that the French are cowards."*

Apart from the personal trauma revealed in his statement, La Vérendrye's concern for portraying an image of bravery is significant. The French Canadians were a mere handful in the midst of thousands of Indians and it was essential they develop a reputation for courage and valor. However, they must have a had a good measure of both to start with or they wouldn't have been where they were!

La Vérendrye did keep his word, and Jean Baptiste joined the war party of about 700 men as it traveled south to the Warroad River - well named because it was the start of the road to war traveled so often by the Sioux of the prairies and the tribes of the lakes and woods as they battled back and forth for generations. Books written in recent years have made us aware of atrocities of Indians against whites and of whites against Indians. Little has been said, however, about the blood bath caused by Indian against Indian. War parties of this size were literally small armies. In this case, the objective of the war party was apparently the villages in the Red Lake area of Minnesota. Jean Baptiste did return safely, but, as we shall soon see, only to meet the fate most feared by his father.

The route the war party had traveled to Minnesota was also used as the beginning of a summer route to Lake Winnipeg. After traveling south on the Warroad River, they would take about a ten-mile portage to Hay River, which fed into the Roseau River. From here they would travel to the Red River, then north to Lake Winnipeg.

In May of 1734, the two scouts who had been sent to Lake Winnipeg returned with their report and recommendations for the site of the new fort. They had seen much but the exciting part of their report was what they had *heard* from the Indians. They had been told that the sea was only a short distance away and easily reached. La Verendrye decided the time had come him to return east and report first-hand these latest developments. No doubt he hoped to solicit further financial support from the merchants of Montreal and possibly even win some contribution from the French government. Before leaving, he instructed one of his men, a man named Cartier, to take a contingent west to Lake Winnipeg and build the third fort at the mouth of the Red River. Tradition has located the site as a few miles below Selkirk on the banks of the Red River. It was later moved to the north bank of the Winnipeg River. Once constructed, the fort was named Maurepas, for the French Colonial Minister.

On his way east, **La Verendrye** met his nephew returning to St. Charles. He gave him authorization to replace his son as commandant; Jean Baptiste, in turn, was to join the crew in the process of constructing the new fort.

La Verendrye seemed always to have been in financial difficulty. This time he was unable to completely regain the faith of the Montreal merchants. However, a compromise was reached and the merchants agreed to finance his work, providing he turned the three forts over to them and they could send some men along to look out for their financial interests. From the point of view of the historian, this was not all bad; it gave La Verendrye more time to explore.

When he returned to Lake of the Woods in the summer of 1735, he brought with him his youngest son, Louis-Joseph, who had been studying mathematics and map making in Quebec. He also brought with him a new priest, Father Jean Pierre Alneau, for whom the largest peninsula in Sabaskong Bay is named today. The young priest (thirty years of age at this point) had arrived from France only the year before. He had actually finished his seminary training in Quebec. Young Alneau was one of seven recruited by New World Bishop Dosquit from his homeland. He left behind a wealthy, widowed mother and sailed with a premonition he would never see her again. Surviving the voyage to the new world was an achievement in itself. Twenty died during the eighty-day journey - (credited by some as a record for the *longest* time to cross the Atlantic by commercial vessel). Storms, disease, and a plague of lice were very nearly too much.

We know from his letters that Father Alneau was a very devout man who really loved his God. He was not an adventurer; he was a missionary. In Quebec he met and talked with every priest who returned from a frontier post that winter; concerning them he wrote,

"... *the striking example they have given me of zeal, recollectedness, self-denial and interior union with God has, through our Lord's mercy awakened in my*

Voyageurs with goods and passengers.
Courtesy Public Archives of Canada
The passengers look worried enough to have been the businessmen sent by the Montreal investors to look out for their interests.

heart a true and sincere desire to make every effort I can to imitate them."

To his superior, Father Bonin, he wrote,

"After all, what the issue of all these projects will be is known to God alone, and, who can tell, perhaps instead of receiving the announcement of the realization of these plans, you may hear the news of my death . . I place all in God's hands. I am disposed to offer Him with a light heart the sacrifice of my life."

"Doubtless I shall have to undergo many hardships; they would have been more than welcome had it been advisable to give me another Jesuit as a companion; but I am to be sent alone among these tribes whose languages as well as whose manner of living is unknown. It was not without much pain that I brought myself to obey. May God accept the sacrifice I make of my life and of all human consolations as expiation for my sins. I shall be separated by several hundred leagues from any other priest, and in that lies the greatest hardship of all my mission. But God seems to require of me the sacrifice of even this consolation. I can refuse Him nothing; may His name be blessed forever!"

"In this country we should set little value on our own lives which are so often in danger. I should deem myself happy if I should be judged worthy of laying my life down for the One from whom I received it."

Father Alneau was given a special assignment in accompanying La Vérendrye. He was to seek out a legendary tribe of Indians who were reported to live in caves rather than wander from place to place as did other tribes. Reports of these Indians had reached Fort St. Charles the previous year. They were called "Quant Chipouanis" - "those who dwell in holes". Actually, the young priest never did find this tribe, and we are not certain they really did exist. Some historians believe, however, that the reports may have had reference to the Mandans who sometimes lived in caves along the river banks in the Dakotas. The Mandans were a unique people in many ways. Not only were they more inclined to settle in one area, but their dwellings were more sophisticated than those of other tribes. By tradition, fair skinned, blue-eyed people lived among them. This was never verified by white explorers, because these light skinned Indians reportedly died from some plague before white man could confirm the legend. Some who believe in the authenticity of the Kensington Ruenstone[1] (found near Kensington, Minnesota) also believe that the fair-skinned Mandans were descendants of the Vikings described on the stone.

Another reason Father Alneau was chosen for this particular assignment was so that he could learn the Indian dialects that he might teach them in their own tongue. We know that he learned quickly, and within a few months was doing just that. We also know that most of the French explorers and voyageurs also learned the Indian languages; this is doubtless another important reason for the usually good relations between the French and Indians.

With the passing of another winter, two of La Vérendrye's sons who had spent the cold months at Lake Winnipeg returned with the news that La Jemeraye was no more. La Vérendrye's able nephew thus became the first recorded white man to die in the West. Although La Vérendrye marked the burial place on a map, the chart has been lost and the exact location of his grave is uncertain. Some historians say it is at the mouth of the Red River, others believe it is where the Roseau River runs into the Red River.

The summer of 1736 was a difficult one at Fort St. Charles. The wild rice had been flooded out the year before; they were generally short of provisions; the supply of gunpowder was dangerously low; and the Sioux were known to again be active on the lake and "looking for scalps". Expected provisions from the East had not arrived. The situation was so serious that La Vérendrye called a meeting of his men (still about fifty in number), and the decision was made to send a small party back to Mackinac Island for relief. This would also mean "fewer mouths to feed" at the fort.

THE MASSACRE

Once the decision had been made the only question was who would go and how many. Father Alneau decided to take advantage of this opportunity to report to his superiors. Perhaps he felt the need for counsel and encouragement. During the long, lean winter he had written,

> "As for the Indians who dwell here, I do not believe, unless it is by a miracle, that they can ever be persuaded to embrace the faith; for even not taking into account the fact that they have no fixed abode, and that they wander about the forests in isolated bands, they are superstitious and morally degraded to a degree beyond conception. In adition both the English and the French, by their accursed avarice, have given them a taste for brandy and this traffic in liquor with the Indians has brought about the destruction of several flourishing missions, and has induced many an Indian to cast away every semblance of religion. This practice constitutes one of the greatest crosses the missionaries have to endure here among the Indians."

It was Father Alneau who requested that La Vérendrye designate his oldest son, Jean Baptiste, to lead the party. It was decided that nineteen others be added to complete the crew. La Vérendrye said in his journal that he chose the best. Many, or possibly all, were soldiers of France. If not soldiers, then voyageurs.

It is easy to speculate as to the exhilaration which must have filled the hearts of those chosen for the trip. There had been months of inactivity at the fort; food supplies, other than those gleaned from the environment, were in short supply; and here was an opportunity to break the routine and return to friends and love ones - even if for a

---

[1] Generally not accepted as authentic by historians.

short time - with whom they could share their adventures hour after hour. On the other hand, La Vérendrye was burdened. Conditions at the fort were not good; relief supplies were needed soon; and rumors of new outbreaks of aggression by the Sioux gave him cause to be concerned about not only the welfare of the fort and its occupants, but also of his son, Father Alneau, and the nineteen men who made up the crew.

The morning of June 5, 1736, was spent in final preparation. Three canoes, each large enough to hold seven men and their gear, were lined up on the beach. Those who were to remain, no doubt, gave the travelers many letters and messages for families and friends in the East, or perhaps even in France itself. La Vérendrye, like any father, had many admonitions for his son. Although it was a large party - large enough to make any band of Sioux think twice before attacking - he was worried. And yet, he had good reason to have faith in his son. Jean Baptiste was well seasoned in the ways of the wilderness; he had traveled the route before; he had earned the commission of a Lieutenant; and he knew the ways of the Indians well - after all, he had even been a member of a war party into Minnesota. Yet, to the father, his son must have seemed very much a boy; he was only twenty-three.

It was afternoon before they were underway. The campsite that first night was about eighteen miles[1] from the fort. If tradition is correct, the location of the island they chose indicates that the route they used in those days may not have been across Big Traverse and up Rainy River. Although there is little doubt the Lake of the Woods was discovered by the Rainy River route and we know it was the route first used by La Vérendrye, it is believed by several historians that the Indians taught the explorers a better way: due east from Massacre Island through sheltered passages between the Alneau Peninsula and Big Island, then the full length of Sabaskong Bay into Lake Kakabikitchiwan, and from there southeast through a series of small lakes and portages to the north bay of Rainy Lake. This avoided the thirty-mile open stretch of Big Traverse. It also made it unnecessary to paddle against the current of the Rainy River and its rapids and waterfalls.

The campsite for these brave men[2] (if tradition is correct) is about three-quarters of a mile in length and one-fourth of a mile wide. It is bisected by a deep ravine which runs from north to south. The western part of the island if rocky, hill-like, and relatively open; the other half is lower ground, brushy, and more heavily timbered.

It was on this tiny island in the heart of the Canadian wilderness, many miles from their homes, that twenty-one very brave men met a violent death at the hands of the Sioux.

It is probable that the men had a meal but we will never know if they saw sleep that night. Neither is it known if the attack came before dark, at night, or at daybreak. We really don't know whether the attack was a complete surprise or an open charge. Tradition has it that the massacre was an act of treachery and that the Sioux had approached the island in the guise of peace and at some signal jumped the men. It is believed that the attack was by a large party of Indians; La Vérendrye's journals spoke of reports of large parties on the lake before and after the massacre. The arrangement of the bodies would indicate that there was no time to flee and that all were killed on the one end of the island. We do know that the Frenchmen fought back; although no

---

[1] LaVerendrye said "seven leagues".

[2] There is a body of evidence that questions the present Massacre Island as the proper site. However, Indians have long considered the traditional island as taboo. Underwater explorations have neither confirmed nor discredited the site.

Indian bodies were found on the island, some hastily buried remains and bloody canoes were found shortly after the massacre on sand beaches on another part of the lake (Muskeg Bay).

La Vérendrye became more worried when seven days after the party's departure, two Indians arrived at Fort St. Charles and told how one of La Vérendrye's men, Bourassa (not one of the twenty-one), had almost met death at the hands of the Sioux. This was confirmed in a letter received two days later from Bourassa himself. He was apparently about to be burned at the stake when an old Indian woman intervened. She had been befriended by the French.[1]

A few days later, the long-expected party from Montreal arrived at St. Charles. When they reported that they had not met the three canoes heading east, La Vérendrye dispatched a search team with instructions to follow the same route. They returned on the 22nd with the tragic news. They had found the bodies of the nineteen murdered crewmen arranged in a circle, and the remains of young **La Vérendrye** and Father Alneau were in the center of that circle. They reported to the fort that -

> *"the heads had been placed on beaver robes, most of them scalped. Father Alneau had one knee upon the ground, an arrow in his side, his head split open, his left hand against the ground, his right hand raised. The Sieur de La Verendrye was lying on his face, his back all scored with knife cuts, a stake thrust into his side, headless, his body ornamented with the leggings and armpieces of porcupine."*

Later in the summer, a group of Indians from Sault St. Marie area (Chippewa) who were friendly to the French, came upon the island and piled bolders over the remains of the two leaders. Because of the period of great tension which followed (the Chippewa were begging **La Vérendrye** to lead them in a war of revenge against the Sioux) the bodies were not retrieved until September. La Vérendrye wrote in his journal,

> *"On September 17th I dispatched the Sergeant with six men to go and raise the bodies of Rev. Father Alneau and my son and on the 18th I had them buried in the chapel, together with the heads of the Frenchmen killed, which they also brought in accordance with my orders."*

We also know that shortly after the massacre, friendly Indians reported seeing twenty blood-stained Sioux canoes in Muskeg Bay, along with two French canoes. The third canoe was found later near the island. The Commandant of Fort Lepin told how in September an Indian chief came into the fort wearing the silver seal of Father Alneau as an ear ring. The chief simply laughed when he was asked where he got it. In an impulse of rage, the Frenchman attacked the Indian and the chief left the stockade, short not only the ornament, but also his ear! Indian lore has told about the massacre down through succeeding generations, and the island itself was taboo for many years. According to legend, Father Alneau's chalice came into the hands of a widowed Sioux woman. She was the proud mother of seven young braves. Shortly after receiving the chalice, she saw her sons, one by one, die horrible deaths. The legend concludes that she blamed the chalice and cast it into one of the rivers which flows into Lake of the Woods.

---

[1] *There are so many tales of men being saved by Indian women, one has to wonder if they didn't have considerably more influence on their men than one would first suspect from our knowledge of their definite second-class status in those days. We know the Indian women carried far more than their fair share of the work load in the family and tribe and that they had practically no voice in the affairs of the community. Yet, we read earlier about the Indian woman who saved the life of young Radisson and that it was the Indian women who shamed and heckled 700 Cree braves into a battle expedition to Red Lake.*

FORT ST. CHARLES AFTER THE MASSACRE

La Verendrye had not had an easy life, and this tragic blow of losing his eldest son, his missionary, and nineteen of his best, would have destroyed lesser men. But La Verendrye did not give up, even though conditions in and around the fort grew worse. The Sioux, flush with victory, were boasting that they would drive all white men out of the country. The Crees, the Ojibway, and the Monsonis, truly friendly Indians, became so taken up with fighting the Sioux that there was little time for trapping and trading furs. La Verendrye's relations with the Montreal merchants were deteriorating, finally forcing him to return east. In the summer of 1737, he set out with fourteen canoes, loaded with furs. He was successful in enlisting support for another expedition but not without considerable difficulty.

Meanwhile, his sons had remained in the West at different forts. However, on August 31, 1738, they all met once again at Fort St. Charles. After doing his best to make sure that his three forts were left in capable hands, La Verendrye embarked on an historic exploration of the area farther west. He traveled the territories of the Assiniboine, the Saskatchewan, and the Mandans. He did not get as far as the mountains but saw a good deal of the western plains. Some sources credit him with getting as far as the Black Hills and the Big Horns. A new fort (Fort La Reine) was established on the Assiniboine, the location of present-day Portage La Prairie. This became the new center of trading, replacing Fort St. Charles as the principal fort. La Verendrye's son, Pierre, was left in command of Fort St. Charles, but there is no record of how long he remained there. In fact, it is not known how long the fort remained in use. No doubt it was retained as a stopping place for a number of years on the route to the forts farther west. We know that La Verendrye's sons moved west with the activity and *may* have explored as far as the Rocky Mountains. La Verendrye, himself, returned once more to Montreal, in 1743. Here, he spent several years defending his name against merchants, government officials and jealous colleagues. Once again, he won the battle and was reappointed "Commander of the Western Forts". He was again organizing an expedition when he died unexpectedly on December 5, 1749, at the age of sixty-four.

Pierre La Verendrye was the last of the great French explorers. He and his sons made a major contribution to the opening of the west. When he began his work, Lake of the Woods and everything west were legend. Fifteen years later, the main water routes had been discovered, explored, and mapped, including Lake of the Woods, Lake Winnipeg, Lake Dauphin, Lake Winnipegosis, Lake Manitoba and the Saskatchewan River. Pierre Gaultier de La Verendrye was a true giant of the North.

VERIFICATION

Captain Jacques Saint-Pierre was appointed as La Verendrye's successor the year following his death (1750). He served three years. His successor was named La Corne. This is the last record we have of a Fort Commandant. However, in 1775 Alexander Henry traveled to Lake of the Woods and visited Fort St. Charles. He described it as "an old French trading house . . . almost entirely destroyed by the Nadowessies (Sioux)."

When Fort St. Charles had fully served its purpose and was abandoned (perhaps sometime after Canada was given up to England by the French in the Treaty of Paris, 1763), it was reclaimed by the wilderness. It does not take the wilderness long to reclaim its own. What appears to be virgin shoreline on the Lake of the Woods today, may in truth at sometime in the past have been an Indian village site, a trading post, or a trapper's cabin. The location of Fort St. Charles was soon forgotten and the wilderness covered the scene of triumph and tragedy with a blanket of grass, moss, brush, and timber. It was not until 1908 that a search party organized by the St. Boniface (Manitoba) Historical Society found the exact location.

An earlier expedition in 1902, led by Archbishop Langevin of St. Boniface, believed they had discovered the fort site on the Canadian side of the Northwest Inlet. They based their explorations on the stories of two aged Indian Chiefs, Powassin and Andagamigowinini, whom they met at Flag Island. The chiefs said there were mounds on both sides of the inlet, which, by Indian lore, were the remains of French structures of some kind. They uncovered the remains of a building on the Canadian side and returned home quite satisfied that this was indeed the site of Fort St. Charles. The Bishop, in reflection, was not satisfied. He returned to Lake of the Woods but failed to find any evidence which would erase his doubts. The detailed descriptions found in La Vérendrye's journals and Father Alneau's letters had not been satisfied.

In 1908, Bishop Langevin organized a third expedition. Because he had been called to Rome, he placed the group under the leadership of Father Paquin. After another false start on the Canadian side, it was decided to explore Magnuson's Island on the American side of the inlet. The remains of fire places, stumps of posts preserved in clay, and other artifacts convinced them they had, in fact, now found the real site. Careful digging unearthed the remains of twelve skeletons, but they were looking for more than this. After all, La Vérendrye's journals had stated that he had ordered the bodies of the priest and his son and the heads of the nineteen crewmen buried in the chapel. However, before they were able to uncover additional relics they were scheduled to return to Winnipeg for a Jesuit retreat. As soon as this was over, they returned to the island and continued their careful digging. Five days later the search was completed. Nineteen skulls were found carefully arranged in two rows, and within the rotted outline of a box lay the headless skeletons of Father Alneau and Jean Baptiste La Vérendrye whose body was identified by a deep cut in the sacrum, caused by the "hoe-like" weapon; the priest's skeleton was identified by a Jesuit Rosary and cassock hook found nearby. The remains were all removed to St. Boniface College near Winnipeg, where they were ironically and tragically lost in a fire which destroyed that institution in 1921.

Other relics were found on the fort site including a chisel, door latch, scissors, iron handles, a tinder box, etc. Hearthstones still showed the ashes of fires which had burned out two hundred years before. The general dimensions of the structure proved to be 60' x 100'; this conforms to the description of the fort as recorded in government papers and Father Alneau's letter. Actually, all evidence of the northside of the fortification had been destroyed by the higher water level caused by the dam at the north end of the lake.

Massacre Island had been identified earlier (1890) by a party of Jesuit priests[1] Their expedition was inspired by the discovery of some of Father Alneau's letters to his mother when a descendant read them and recognized their significance.

---

[1]*The identification of Massacre Island is not considered positive by some sources. It could well be that we will never know for certain on which island the massacre took place.*

CHAPTER II
Lake of the Woods Under a New Master - England

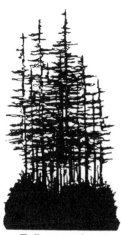

It is somewhat surprising that we know so much more about the Lake of the Woods history during the first century after its discovery than we do about the next 100 years. This fact underscores our indebtedness to Pierre La Vérendrye and his meticulous journal keeping, the records of the Church of France, and the rediscovered letters of Father Alneau.

Following the death of La Vérendrye in 1749, his sons and their compatriots continued to travel the Lake of the Woods on their way back and forth between Montreal and the new western outposts. The French still dominated the lake and controlled the fur trade of the area. But wars fought on far-off battle fields were to have profound effect on the history of Lake of the Woods. The Peace of Paris, signed in 1763, ending the Seven Years War, marked the temporary end of hostilities between England and France, but deeded the Canadian part of North America east of the Mississippi to England. The English-chartered Hudson's Bay Company was to become the dominant influence. But the French did not give up easily. Come British rule or not, they were in Canada to stay. In fact, the French voyageurs were destined to service the area well into the eighteen hundreds. But as we shall see, it was a losing battle and it was inevitable that British influence, as represented by the Hudson's Bay Company, would eventually control this whole area.

Hudson's Bay Company
INCORPORATED 2ND MAY 1670

Although the Hudson's Bay Company was chartered in 1670 by Charles I of England, it did not establish any posts or operations in the Lake of the Woods area until sometime after the passing of La Vérendrye. However, his journals tell us that the mammoth trading company did have some effect on this area even in his day in that La Vérendrye found the Indians had in their possession firearms and other weapons as well as miscellaneous metal utensils which had been acquired in trading with the Hudson's Bay Company northern posts - perhaps as far north as Hudson Bay itself. At the outset, the company operated several posts on the southwest shores of the Bay. The Indians brought their furs to these posts and travel by the English traders was unnecessary. But, as the supply of furs was reduced in that area and as the French continued to develop trade with the Indians in the area south of Hudson Bay, the British were finally forced to penetrate the wilderness. The water routes from Lake Superior westward fell into relative disuse after the passing of **La Verendrye**, but by the end of the 18th century the French-Canadian voyageurs were on the scene. As the Hudson's Bay operators moved into the area, conflict was inevitable.

One of the first, if not the first, Hudson's Bay Posts in this area was constructed on the Rainy River at Manitou Falls in 1793 by John McKay. This preceeded by only one year a post developed for the company by Thomas Norn in 1794 at the mouth of the Rainy River. The post at Kenora (Rat Portage) was not developed until 1836, but

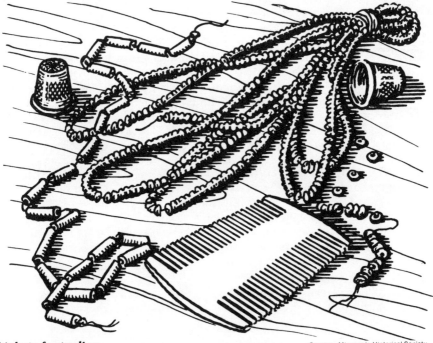

Trinkets for trading.   Courtesy Minnesota Historical Society

eventually became the most important Hudson's Bay operation on Lake of the Woods. The post on the Northwest Angle also came later.

The trappers who did not work for the Hudson's Bay Co. soon found (here as elsewhere in Canada) that they were no match for the well-financed English company, so they merged themselves into a competitive organization known as the North West Company. The fur trade industry was highly profitable, which only added "fuel to the fire". The area between Lake Superior and the Red River became one of the major scenes of the bloody rivalry. Even the Indians were drawn into the conflict. The rivalry grew so intense and expensive that the two big fur trading organizations finally merged in 1821 into a combination known thereafter as "The Hudson's Bay Company."

In 1869-70 the Company relinquished to the Canadian Government much of the authority granted in its original charter of 1670. In return it received 300,000 pounds and fifteen million acres of land which was to be selected in various parts of Canada.

The Lake of the Woods was included in the district known as "Lac La Pluie", meaning "Lake of Rain". The following lands were chosen as a part of the settlement and were listed in the annual report of the Hudson's Bay Company in 1872 -

Fort Alexander	500 acres
Fort Frances	500 acres
Eagles Nest	20 acres
Big Island	20 acres
Lac du Bonnet	20 acres
Lake of the Woods	50 acres
Whitefish	20 acres
English River	20 acres
Hungry Hall	20 acres
Front Lake	20 acres
Rat Portage	20 acres
Shoal Lake	20 acres
Clear Water Lake	20 acres
Sandy Point	20 acres

Of all these trading posts, only the one at Lac du Bonnet remains in operation (under the Northern Stores Division of H B C) and so far as it could be determined in contacts with the Company, no property has been retained by the company at any of the other sites.

Although little is known today about many of the posts listed, the Hudson's Bay Company provided the following information:

The Eagles Nest Post was located on Eagle Lake about 75 miles east of Kenora; it was opened in 1860 and closed about twenty years later.

The Big Island operation was small; it opened in 1865 but no closing date information is available.

Lac du Bonnet, the post which remains in operation, is located on the Winnipeg River near the present townsite of the same name.

The post described as "Lake of the Woods" was apparently a small operation on the west side of the lake but other than that no details are available.

"Whitefish" probably refers to an operation on Whitefish Bay of Lake of the Woods.

Shoal Lake was the site of an apparently small and shortlived operation.

Clear Water Lake House was a small post located on what is now called Teggau Lake.

Hungry Hall, near the mouth of the Rainy River.

Fort Frances, at the site of the present city by that name on the Rainy River.

Fort Alexander, at the site of the former North West Fur Trading Company post near the mouth of the Winnipeg River (south bank).

Rat Portage, present day Kenora and Keewatin.

The following information furnished by the Company gives us considerable insight into life at these outposts, the conflict between H B C and the North West Company, and the general impact of the huge trading company on Lake of the Woods history.

FORT FRANCES

As early as 1777 the Hudson's Bay Company was anxious to establish a post on Rainy Lake, but at that time the area was not known to Company employees. It was not until the summer of 1791 that Donald MacKay on one of his inland journeys marked a site for a fort on Rainy River, not far from the entrance to Rainy Lake.

John McKay arrived at this place in September, 1793, but he considered the site marked by Donald MacKay as being unsuitable, so he eventually built his post just below Manitou Falls on Rainy River about 32 miles from the North West Company Fort* (situated near the entrance of Rainy Lake). The H B C post was dismantled in October, 1795, and John McKay went to settle at the mouth of Rainy River. This post was abandoned in the summer of 1797, and the Company did not return to the Rainy Lake area until 1816.

Donald MacPherson of the H B C in a report dated "Lake la Pluie" May 30, 1818, states that he arrived at Rainy Lake from Fort William on November 5, 1816, and found that the North West Company had handed over their fort to the H B C employees. On the instructions of Lord Selkirk, MacPherson took charge of this post on behalf of the Hudson's Bay Company. (Selkirk had captured the North West Company's headquarters at Fort William and its post at Rainy Lake after hearing of the massacre of Governor Semple and his followers at Seven Oakes, in present-day Winnipeg).

On the union of the Hudson's Bay and North West Companies in 1821, Nicholas Garry, governor of the Hudson's Bay Company, visited a number of posts, and he arrived at Rainy Lake July 27, 1821. The following extract is taken from his diary:

> ". . . at 2 o'clock we started and after running a Rapid we entered the River of Rainy Lake . . . At a quarter before three we arrived at the Portage de Chaudiere which is about 400 paces and is made to avoid a very fine Waterfall. On an Eminence close to the Fall is the Hudson's Bay Post commanding a most beautiful and picturesque Situation. The North West Post is about a mile higher* up the River. The Post of Lac La Pluie or Rainy Lake before the Union of the two Companies was one of great importance. Here the people from Montreal came to meet those who arrived from the Athabascan Country and exchange Lading with them receiving the Furs and giving the Goods to trade in return. It will now become a mere trading Post as the Athapascans will be supplied from York Fort . . ."

*It was lower down the river.

After the Union of the two companies it was the Fort belonging to the H B C which was occupied.

On or about February 24, 1830, Governor George Simpson married his cousin, Frances Ramsey Simpson. He took his bride to the Red River Settlement and on the way passed the post at Rainy Lake. Their arrival is recorded by Chief Factor J.D. Cameron in his journal as follows:

> 1830 June 1 "Tuesday arrived about 11 o'clock Governor Simpson accompanied by a young lovely and accomplished Lady whom he married shortly before he left London . . . They were all off before 5 o'clock p.m. . . . .".

The Hudson's Bay Company's post was always known as "Lac la Pluie" post until September 25, 1830, when Chief Factor J.D. Cameron recorded the change of name in his journal as follows:

> 1830 Sept. 25 "Saturday. Fine Weather. This morning at Sunrise the New flag staff was up, and the new flag hoisted - In the Meantime a flaccon of Spirits was broken & spilled on the foot of the Staff, at the fort named Fort Frances in honor of Mrs. Simpson's Christian name. All the Whites gave three Hearty Cheers - and the Indians fired above 300 Shots."

On October 7, 1874, a fire broke out at Fort Frances and destroyed some of the buildings which were very old and closely huddled together. The destroyed buildings were replaced and the post continued as a fur trade post until 1897-98 when, owing to the opening up of the country around Fort Frances, it was no longer possible to carry on the fur trade business there and the post was consequently transferred from the Fur Trade Department to the Saleshop Department. This Saleshop continued to operate until it was destroyed by fire on February 2, 1903.

HUDSON'S BAY COMPANY OUTPOST AT THE MOUTH OF THE RAINY RIVER

John McKay built the first post in the Rainy River area for the Hudson's Bay Company in 1793. It was located below Manitou Fall. This post was dismantled in 1795 and McKay went to settle at the mouth of Rainy River where Thomas Norn had built a post in 1794. This post was abandoned in 1797 as McKay and his men were transferred to the Red River area. In August 1793 John Cobb of the Hudson's Bay Company left Osnaburgh for "Mr. McKay's House" but when he arrived on September 20 he found that the North West Company had pillaged everything and burnt the men's house. He wintered at Ash Falls.

The post at the mouth of the Rainy River was again occupied during the winter of 1826-27. So far the name given to this Hudson's Bay Company post at the mouth of Rainy River has not been mentioned in Company documents. The first reference to it being called "Hungry Hall" is during the trading season of 1832-33. The following account is taken from "The Great Lone Land" by W.F. Butler:

"... on the 31st July (1870) we stood away from the Portage du Rat into the Lake of the Woods. I had added another man to my crew, which now numbered seven hands, the last accession was a French half-breed, named Morrisseau ...we were running through a vast expanse of marsh and reeds into the mouth of Rainy River; the Lake of the Woods was passed, and now before me lay eighty miles of the Rivere-de-la-Pluie . . . About five miles from the mouth of Rainy River there was a small out-station of the Hudson's Bay Company kept by a man named Morrisseau, a brother of my boatman. It was a place so wretched-looking that its name of Hungry Hall seemed well adapted to it."

Captain Hushe, who was attached to Colonel Wolseley's Expedition recorded that he left Fort Frances on August 10, 1870, and on the next day approached the mouth of Rainy River. He continued:

"In the wide reaches of the river the strong westerly wind blowing against the current produced a rough chopping sea, against which we rowed hard for three hours, till we came to a small Hudson's Bay post, two miles from the mouth of the river, where we were glad to stop for breakfast . . . The little post at which we breakfasted is kept by a half-breed named Morrison, and is called "Hungry Hall . . ."

George M. Grant, in his book, "Ocean to Ocean" recorded traveling down Rainy River on July 27, 1872, and added:

"Of the seventy-five miles of Rainy River, down which we sailed today, every mile seemed well adapted for cultivation and the dwellings of men. At eleven o'clock the moon rose; at half-past twelve we reached Hungry Hall, a post of the Hudson Bay Company and a village of wigwams . . ."

In 1886 Hungry Hall consisted of two buildings, a trading shop 20 x 16, 1½ story high, and a dwelling house of 35 x 17, 1½ story high. Hungry Hall was closed during outfit of 1892-93. (An outfit ran from June 1 to May 31)

FORT ALEXANDER · 1795

One of La Verendrye's sons established Fort Maurepas on the north bank of the Winnipeg River, near its mouth, in 1734. Troussaint Lesieur, NorWester, built a post, Bas de la Riviere, on the south bank in 1792, and in 1794 Duncan McGillivray records his arrival "at the Fort near the bottom of the River (Winnipeg)." Edward Clouston of the Hudson's Bay Company traveled from Osnaburgh in 1795 to establish a house near the mouth of the Winnipeg River, operated until 1802, and known as Point au Foutre. Daniel W. Harmon visited the place in 1800 and stated that both companies operated posts near the mouth of the Winnipeg River. Writing of his travels in 1798, David Thompson says that where the Winnipeg River flows "into Lake Winnipeg is a trading house first established by the French and kept up by the North West Company in Latitude 50.37.46N Longitude 95.39.34W Variation nine degrees east". Thompson adds that "The greatest use of the Winnepeg House is for a depot of Provisions, which are brought to this place by the canoes and boats from the Bison countries of the Red and Saskatchewan Rivers, and distributed to the canoes and boats for the voyages to the several wintering fur trading Houses." Gabriel Franchere visited the North West Company fort at the mouth of the Winnipeg River in 1814 and writes:

"This trading post has more the air of a large and well cultivated farm, than of a fur trader's factory; a neat and elegant mansion, built on a slight eminence, and sourrounded by barley, peas, oats and potatoes."

There was no Hudson's Bay Company post here during the trading season prior to the Union, but the Company has operated this post continuously from 1821 to 1941. From 1821-31 it was the headquarters of the Winnipeg River District. Then it became part of Rainy Lake District, Red River and later Lake Winnipeg District.

The Hudson's Bay Company Fort Alexander was on the site of the North West Company post on the south bank of the river. After the Union, supplies and returns came and went by Norway House, and the Fort Alexander to Fort William route fell into disuse.

(end of quote from Hudson's Bay Co. records)

THE VOYAGEURS - heroes of the second century of Lake of the Woods history.

Fur trading was adventurous enough in itself, but the voyageurs added real color, drama and excitement to the century following La Verendrye's explorations. Even though the British were destined to be the dominant force in this area through the influence of the Hudson's Bay Company, it was the French-Canadian voyageurs who have captured our hearts and our imaginations with their colorful dress, their swift canoes, the singing of the gay chansons of France, and their spectacular fetes of courage and physical endurance. In all history, they are unequaled in the transportation of furs and trading supplies.

The English and Scots used some canoes but also developed their own kind of boat. They were wooden, double-prowed, over-sized row boats which varied between 28 and 40 feet in length. They were named "York boats" - after York Factory, the Hudson Bay trading post where they were manufactured. Most of the men who manned these boats were experienced oarsmen from the islands off the north coast of Scotland (called Orkneymen). Although clumsy in appearance when compared to the canoes of the Indians and voyageurs, they proved practical and durable on the larger

Courtesy Allied Van Lines

A Hudson's Bay Co. York Boat - practical and durable on the larger rivers and on open waters.

rivers and on open waters. But somehow, the Scots and Englishmen who propelled these York boats lacked the color and romantic flair of the French Canadians with their swift canoes. In each case, the men and their vessels were well matched.

The early voyageurs did not have to depend on trial and error to find their way west. They probably made good use of charts and maps developed by the explorers about whom we have been reading. In addition, we have pointed out how well the French got along with the Indians. They befriended them, intermarried with them, and generally accepted them as equals and brothers. In return, the Indians guided them across unknown waters and over portages worn smooth over the centuries by thousands of moccasins.

The rugged climate presented as many problems as the wilderness itself. They could be assured of ice free waters only from approximately May 1 to November 1 in the Lake of the Woods area and less than that in the far north. The North West Company, which was the employer of the voyageurs, was headquartered at Montreal. The westernmost outpost for gathering furs was nearly three thousand miles west at Lake Athabasca. It was impossible to make this journey and return during a single travel season. Therefore, the route was divided into two parts, each traveled by a separate set of voyageurs. One group wintered at Montreal and other villages in that area. They would set out from that city[1] in the spring with their loads of guns, gunpowder, knives, iron stoves,[2] kettles, cooking utensils, sewing instruments, flour, salt, trinkets, blankets, liquors, and many other items for which the Indians would be willing to give up their furs. All goods were bundled in 90 pound packs or crated. A crew of eight to ten men would paddle the 36 foot Montreal canoes. They were made of a cedar strip framework and covered with birchbark. Whole fleets of these canoes would travel together, paddling up the Ottawa River, then the Mattawa River to Trout Lake, then portaging into Lake Nipissing, down the French River to Lake Huron, past Sault St. Marie, into Lake Superior, and west across that giant body of water arriving at Grand Portage about the end of June.

Meanwhile, when the ice broke up at Lake Athabasca and at the other northern and western outposts, the voyageurs who had wintered at these wilderness locations would load their 25 foot North canoes with the furs that had been acquired over the winter from the Indians. The crew consisted of five or six men. It was imperative that they rendevous at Grand Portage with the voyageurs from the east by mid July or they would not have time to return to the wilderness outposts by freeze-up. The rendezvous at Grand Portage called for a celebration; and the voyageurs knew how to celebrate! It is a wonder that the small fort at Grand Portage survived the thousand or more voyageurs and perhaps twice that many Indians who gathered there each July. There was a great deal of rivalry, though usually good natured, between the "men of the north" as the voyageurs from the west called themselves, and those from Montreal who were nicknamed "pork eaters" by their counterparts. There was no domestic meat to be enjoyed by the "men of the north" in those days, only wild game. The "hommes du nord" considered themselves at least a little more hardy than the men from the East who spent each winter in the comforts of their homes. Then, too, they had farther to travel and faced a more uncertain wilderness in the West.

When the rendezvous was over, the "pork eaters" loaded their freight canoes with furs and headed for Montreal. Their counterparts picked up their 90 pound bales of hardware and headed up the rugged, nine-mile portage to the Pigeon River. The

---

[1] *Actually a few miles up stream at Lachine - in order to avoid rapids.*
[2] *Not usually for trade but rather for trappers' cabins.*

Trading goods from the voyageurs' packs.

Courtesy Hudson's Bay Co.

"Pork eaters" Leaving Lachine for Grand Portage [Lake Superior]

Voyageurs considered this experience as one which separated "the men from the boys" and used it as a proving ground for their strength and endurance. Wagers and challenges characterized the portage. Each man was expected to carry eight - 90 pound bales (usually two at a time). However, as a bonus for anything over that load, they were paid one Spanish dollar per bale. A normal load of two bales at a time meant a total of 72 miles of portage, so the stronger men would try to take more. The record haul was reported to be a wager won by a voyageur who carried 820 pounds (more than nine bales) uphill for one mile! And the portage must have seemed all uphill since the spot where they came out on the Pigeon River is about 650 feet above the level of Lake Superior.

From the Pigeon River, the voyageurs trail led to Lakes Saganaga, Basswood, Lac La Croix, and Rainy. It is likely that the voyageurs used Rainy River rather than the alternate route described in the Massacre Island saga, at least while going with the current on the way west. Regardless of the route, all voyageurs crossed the Lake of the Woods and then passed north up the Winnipeg River to Lake Winnipeg itself. Many voyageurs went much father west; some to the most westward post: Fort Chipewyan on Lake Athabasca.

It is exciting to realize that some of the towering white and Norway pines we see today, looked down on the colorful voyageurs of more than 100 years ago. A few of

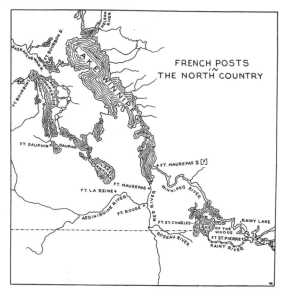

French posts in the North Country (18th Century Map)

these pines, true giants of the north, are our living link with not only the voyageurs, but even the La Verendryes!

JOHN TANNER - The White Indian

Few men can rightfully be called "a legend in their own time", but John Tanner was such a man. Some called him "the White Indian"; the Indians called him "Shaw-Shaw Wa Be-Na-Se", "The Falcon". His life story reads like a movie script.

Born in 1770, the son of a minister, he was kidnapped by the Shawnee at the age of nine from his home along the Kentucky shore of the Ohio River. He was cruelly treated by his captors until adopted by an Ottawa squaw known as Net-No-Kwa, the Otter Woman. Tanner's foster mother was a character in her own right. She was well known by both the Ottawas and the Ojibway. A flag flew from the bow of her canoe and on at least one occasion she rated a salute of guns when her party approached Fort Mackinac.

Net-No-Kwa lost her husband when John was thirteen and her own oldest son was fifteen. She had difficulty supporting her children and wandered westward in search of relatives. Her search was not in vain and she found help in the person of Peshauba, a chief of the Ottawas who had settled on the site of present day Winnipeg. Net-No-Kwa and her family spent three years with Peshauba, sometimes exploring and trapping many miles to the north and west of Winnipeg. At the end of this time, they gathered up their small fortune in furs and headed east for Mackinac, where she felt she would have the best chance to receive fair compensation. However, along the way, traders took advantage of Net-No-Kwa by getting her drunk. According to Tanner, she traded 129 beaver skins and several buffalo robes for rum. In a few days time, the family had nothing to show for three years of hard work. This made a lasting impression on Tanner, and at least partially explains his life-long crusade in behalf of the Indians.

Earl Chapin, in his work in collaboration with the Warroad Historical Society, tells the following story which demonstrates Tanner's fight for Indian rights and fair treatment and his own personal feud with the North West Company:

Since Pierre de La Vérendrye brought trade into this country in 1732, the Indians had received "credits" in goods, advances against their winter's catch of furs. In 1813, Mr. Wells, trader for the North West Company at Pembina, summarily called the Indians together and informed them that he would "not give them credit to the value of a single needle." Having lived for generations on the assumption of an advance of goods, and being naturally improvident, this sudden change of policy put the Indians in desperate straits.

Tanner pleaded the Indians' case, to which Wells replied that the shiftless beggars could freeze or starve, for all he cared.

Tanner bided his time. He took his credit with the Hudson's Bay Company that winter, though the distance to the post at Fort Douglas was great. His first stop with his load of furs that following spring was at Pembina.

When Wells learned that the Falcon had arrived with a large catch he sent word that he wished to see him. After some deliberation, Tanner went to the North West Company post, knowing that this would be a confrontation of the will and authority of both of them.

The factor's excessive cordiality warned Tanner that he was up to some new high-handedness, but the magnitude of it shocked even the Falcon. Into the trading post strode several of Wells' half-breeds, carrying Tanner's winter catch of furs. They walked past the two men and the watching Chippewa, and deposited their load in the trader's bedroom. When they came out, Wells locked the bedroom door.

Had the Falcon followed his inclination, he would have murdered the paunchy trader then and there. But he had a greater responsibility than that. His responsibility was to humble Wells before the Indians, in order to break the yoke of servitude they had accepted.

Slowly the Falcon arose, stretching and loosening his muscles. The trader had a sudden qualm. He looked for reassurance from his breeds, and then, with sudden disquiet, toward the no longer loafing Indians.

Keeping the half breeds in the corner of his eye, Tanner drew his knife, then with an obvious gesture of disdain, flipped it into the floor where it stood quivering.

The Falcon was making his play. It was, he knew, the only way he could gain more than a life for a life; but for that chance he staked his own life without reservation. Tanner was now completely unarmed.

He put his shoulder down and lunged against the bedroom door. There was a splintering of wood as the door smashed in.

Tanner picked up his packs and strode back through the trading room. With a high pitched yelp of indignation, Wells snatched at the Falcon's bundles. A cord broke, scattering furs on the floor. Completely ignoring the trader, the white Indian bent to pick up his peltries. Beside himself with rage, Wells snatched up his pistol and cocked it, shoving it into Tanner's middle. Well's face was flushed, his eyes dilated with excitement. Tanner stood rigid. Wells could feel the hard stomach muscles at the muzzle of his gun. In his excited fancy it seemed that no bullet could pierce them. He looked into the cold gray eyes of this incredible person and they had never seen more like those of a bird of prey than now.

"Why don't you shoot?" the Falcon sneered. The trader's quick passion ebbed under the cold gaze of a man who seemed not quite human. "Are you a squaw, that you do not dare to kill me when you might?"

The spectators at the other end of the room were as taut as bowstrings.

"I think that you are a rabbit and not fit to associate with men," said the Falcon. He was the central and dominating figure on the stage now, an actor choosing his words for their effect upon a special audience.

The Falcon smiled a thin-lipped smile, and Wells suddenly felt his wrist seized and twisted in a grip as excruciating as the taloned grasp of a predator. The pistol fell from his numbed hand and struck the floor, exploding. The ball thudded into the wall.

Still gripping the trader's wrist, the Falcon slapped him across both sides of the face. Wells began to cry for help, bleating like a sheep. The Falcon dropped his quarry and restored the knife to his belt.

"Put him out of the house!" screamed Wells to his half breeds.

"You are as able to that as we," one replied. And there was considerable truth to that.

Tanner beckoned to his Chippewa tribesmen. Without a sidelong glance at the trader or his henchmen, they picked up the scattered furs and carried them out of the post.

An hour before not an Indian would have dared to thus flout the North West Company in its own establishment. But courage was the prime criterion in their primitive thinking. Victory in a knife or gun battle would not have impressed them — they were frequently involved in such when the rum began to flow. The Falcon had chosen the one way to break the Indian's belief in the omnipotence of the North West Company and its representatives. Tanner had bested the company factor in a battle of will and in so doing, reduced Wells' influence among the Chippewa.

(end of quote from Chapin)

Tanner spent one winter in the area of Grygla, Minnesota. This was really a no-man's land between the plains of the Sioux and the lake country of the Ojibway. He knew the country was rich in furs inasmuch as the Indian tribes had not trapped the area because of fear of each other. It took real courage to lead his band of Ojibway so close to the stronghold of the Sioux. They hunted with bows and arrows so as not to be detected, and headquartered in a fortified village they had constructed for protection in case they were found out. From this operation came the expression "Stealing Earth"; later changed to Thief River and Thief Lake.

Tanner was also a soldier of fortune. On June 19, 1816, a feud between the North West Company and the residents of the Scottish settlement of Selkirk (on the Red River near the site of present day Winnipeg) climaxed in the massacre of twenty people, including Robert Semple, the local governor for the Hudson's Bay Company. It became known as the "Seven Oaks Massacre". The employees of the North West

Company (most of them half-Indian and half-white) also seized two Hudson's Bay Posts, Daer at Pembina and Douglas, where the Red and Assiniboine Rivers meet. Lord Alexander Selkirk, the founder of the community that bore his name, wanted revenge. He hired fifty mercenary soldiers from the Napoleonic wars (called De Meurons). Winter set in by the time they reached Rainy Lake and the leadership decided they should not proceed without a guide. John Tanner was recommended as the best. He was promptly hired along with twenty of his braves. As we have seen, Tanner had no love for the North West Company and he was an eager ally.

Because it was winter, the normal route via the Winnipeg River was not practical. Tanner led the seventy men with their two cannon across the Roseau bogs. Fort Daer gave up without a fight, but the well-defended Fort Douglas was not an easy mark. But while the mercenaries were bickering over the best way to take the fort, Tanner and his men, augmented by a few more venturesome Swiss soldiers, scaled the stockade at night, surprised the defenders, and captured the fort. In his gratitude, Lord Selkirk rewarded Tanner with a 20 pound/year stipend for life. He took a deep and personal interest in the Falcon and helped reunite him with his family, whom he had presumed dead.

John Tanner was a religious man. He translated parts of the New Testament into Ojibway and was not afraid to pray when faced with adversity. He related the following experience at a time of great hunger:

"We were all reduced nearly to starvation, and at last I resorted to medicine hunting. Half the night I sang and prayed and then laid down to sleep. I saw, in my dream, a beautiful young man come down through the hole in the top of my lodge, and stand directly before me.

"What," he said, "is this noise and crying I hear? Do I know when you are hungry and in distress? I look upon you and it is not necessary that you call me with such loud cries."

Then, pointing directly to the setting sun he said, "Do you see those tracks?"

"Yes," I answered, "they are the track of two moose."

"I give you those two moose to eat."

He then went out of the door of my lodge and as he raised the blanket I saw the snow was falling rapidly. At the earliest dawn I started from the lodge in a heavy fall of snow, and taking the course pointed out to me, long before noon I fell on the track of two moose and killed them both, a male and a female, and extremely fat."

Much of John Tanner's life was associated with the Lake of the Woods. The valley of the Roseau River was one of his favorite haunts for both trapping and hunting. He also did some farming on Garden Island.

In his latter years, Tanner made an effort to live with his relatives in the East, but was not happy. He returned to Mackinac where he worked as an interpreter for the American Fur Company and later he headquartered at Sault Ste. Marie where he served as a guide for Henry Schoolcraft.

When accused of murdering Schoolcraft's brother he disappeared and was never seen again. He was absolved of the charges when the real murderer confessed, but he never knew his name had been cleared.

A skeleton found in a swamp near Sault Ste. Marie was thought by some to have been Tanner; others believed he had returned to Lake of the Woods or traveled even farther west. Either way, so large a figure deserved a better fate than death in a swamp or hiding out in fear to the last of his days.

THE AMERICAN FUR TRADING COMPANY

The North West Company and the Hudson's Bay Company dominated the Lake of the Woods scene until the international border was established between the United States and Canada. Although the Northwest Angle was not clearly established until 1872[1] the border was roughly drawn by 1821. At that time it became quite clear to the Canadian companies that they had best abandon their posts south of the 49th parallel. The American Fur Trading Company, controlled by John Jacob Astor, fell heir to these posts. In the records of that company, we find the following exerpts from business correspondence:

November 31, 1821: from Ramsay Crooks to his business associate, John Jacob Astor:

"Since the British government has legislated us out of Canada, we shall next year occupy three posts within our lines in the vicinity of Rainy Lake to the Lake of the Woods."

December 5, 1821: Crooks to Robert Stuart, the agent at Mackinac:

"Morrison will next year establish the Rainy Lake country and carry our trade as near as possible to the border line."

1823: from Stuart to Mr. Stone of the Stone, Bostwick Co., which combined with Astor's company in that year:

"Stuart complained about the unfair competition from the Hudson's Bay Company which traded whiskey to the Indians forbidden by our government. At each post [say three in number] . . . we found it impossible to oppose them successfully."

Henry Schoolcraft, the famous explorer of the Mississippi, served for a time as the Indian Agent at Sault Ste. Marie. The south shore of the Lake of the Woods was included in his district. On August 9, 1824, he wrote in a report on trading posts in his agency:

"Pursuant to instructions, I have determined on the following places where trade may be carried on with the different bands within the limits of this agency . . . #18: at Rainy Lake. #19 at War Road."

We can be quite certain that the post at the mouth of the Warroad River was established no later than 1822.

Although the American Fur Trading Company became a respectable rival of the merged Hudson's Bay Company, the international boundary prevented the bloodshed that characterized the old rivalries prior to that time. However, the Indians were free to trade on both sides of the boundary and indications are that the American Company usually came out second best.

---

[1] *The actual point where the Northwest Angle intersected with the shoreline of the Lake was not finally established until 1925.*

CHAPTER III
Rat Portage - Center of
Activity since 1836

"Rat Portage" refers to the general area at the north end of the Lake at the outlet to the Winnipeg River. The Indians named the area "Waszush Unigum", which literally means "the road (portage) to the country of the muskrat". The country along the Winnipeg River for about forty miles north of Lake of the Woods was ideal habitat for muskrats; hence the name "Rat Portage" was given to the access to this area. The French quickly adopted the Indian name and called it "Portage du Rhat". When the Hudson's Bay Company moved into the Lake of the Woods district, it made this area its headquarters and used the English version of the name, simply: Rat Portage.

The Indians also called this area "Keewaydin" - meaning "The North". It can be said, therefore, that the Indians spoke of this area as "the road to the muskrat country at the north end of the lake".

The Hudson's Bay post here became the gathering point for the fur trade industry throughout the Lake of the Woods area. During the second half of the eighteen hundreds, this was the center of activity for the lake, and the community grew in population and importance.

Although "Rat Portage" referred originally to the entire Keewatin-Kenora area, the name was finally given exclusively to the community we now know as Kenora. This came about at the time of the construction of the Canadian Pacific Railroad (1879-1884). It was decided that two post offices should be established. One of these was to be called "Keewatin Mills" (from Keewaydin", meaning north) and the other "Rat Portage". The story has been accepted down through the years that the seals for the two offices were prepared and sent to John Mather, who resided in the tiny village we now call Keewatin, and apparently the decision was his as to which of the two outposts was to receive which name. Any of us faced with the same alternatives would probably have made the same decision; he gave the name "Rat Portage" to the "other village".

We have already seen how the Lake of the Woods was one of the focal points of the conflict between three great fur trading companies; Kenora was also in the center of a conflict between Ontario and Manitoba. The two provincial governments both laid claim to Kenora between the years of 1870 and 1884. The Manitoba government claimed everything west of a line 6½ miles east of present-day Thunder Bay. Yet, Ontario had assumed jurisdiction over this area and had operated a court house and jail and had appointed magistrates in Rat Portage since 1871. A commission was appointed by the Dominion government to arbitrate the dispute and after studying the question ruled in favor of Ontario. However, the Dominion government refused to accept the finding of the commission and in 1881 the Canadian Parliament passed an act honoring the Manitoba claim. From 1881 to 1883 Kenora "enjoyed" two sets of government officials and buildings. Both governments issued licenses and collected fees. Troubles grew worse and reached a climax when E.M. Rideout was arrested by Manitoba authorities for operating a roadhouse under an Ontario license. He was promptly placed in the Manitoba jail. Apparently most residents of the area favored Ontario jurisdiction and soon a full-scale revolt was in process. The Manitoba jail was

Main Street, Rat Portage, 1880   Courtesy Minnesota Historical Society

raided and the prisoners set free. The Manitoba officials in turn were arrested and incarcerated in the Ontario jail!

On September 28, 1883, the residents of Kenora actually were allowed to vote for the election of members to both the Manitoba and Ontario Provincial Legislatures.

Later in the same year, the residents of Rat Portage held a town meeting at which they made formal request to be incorporated as an Ontario village. The next year, in 1884, the dispute was finally settled by the Privy Council of England! The question was decided in favor of Ontario.

When the dispute began in 1870, the Rat Portage-Keewatin area was settled by only a handful of adventurous traders; when the dispute was resolved in 1884, Kenora, alone, had a population of more than 4,500. As we shall see, this remarkable growth of the frontier town was the result of a combination of things: the coming of the railroad in 1881, the beginning of the logging and lumbering industry, and the discovery of gold.

Rat Portage Waterfront, 1880   Courtesy Minnesota Historical Society

CHAPTER IV
The Northwest Angle

ORIGIN

Every schoolboy knows that except for Alaska, the Northwest Angle of Minnesota is the northernmost point of the United States. But few know how it got there! Actually, it was the result of ignorance, compromise, accident, and an astronomer's ruler! Benjamin Franklin, John Adams, and John Jay had important roles in causing the confusion. It is not a little surprising that these fathers of our country even knew the Lake of the Woods existed!

The confusion had its beginning at the Treaty of Paris at the conclusion of the American Revolutionary War (1783), and did not end until the boundary was surveyed and definitely established in 1925 - nearly a century and a half later.

Franklin, Adams, and Jay were among those representing the United States at the Treaty of Paris. After a number of proposals and counter proposals, the British ministry suggested that the boundary follow Rainy River "to the Lake of the Woods, thence through the said lake to the most northwestern part thereof, and from thence on a due west course to the river Mississippi . . ." All this would have been fine except for one "minor detail" - The Mississippi River does not lie west of the Lake of the Woods; in fact, the source of the great river is about 140 miles south of the lake! The negotiators of the treaty had made the mistake of relying on "Mitchell's Map of North America", published in London in 1775. This map showed the Lake of the Woods as an oblong body of water with a regular shoreline and containing nine islands. Furthermore, it showed the Mississippi River as west of the lake. It also showed the Lake draining east to Lake Superior instead of north to Hudson Bay.

Shortly after the signing of the treaty, the British became aware of the problem. As the Treaty of Ghent was being negotiated, they proposed that boundary negotiations be reopened and that the line be redefined from Lake Superior to the Mississippi. The government of the United States acknowledged the problem but said that it was not interested in dropping the border south of Lake of the Woods to the river. Agreement was finally reached, however, on the need to locate the most northwest point on the Lake of the Woods and its relationship to the Mississippi. It is interesting to speculate how a great deal of the history of Canada and the United States (and even the world) might have been changed if the British position had prevailed and the line had been drawn from Lake Superior to the Mississippi, thus giving almost the entire iron range of Minnesota to Canada! The industrial growth and power of the United States would have been seriously stunted without these vast resources.

An international commission was appointed to resolve the problem. However, the surveyors hired to locate the "northwesternmost point" found they could not cope with the irregular shoreline and all of the peninsulas and bays. They actually gave up and reported the impossibility of the task. The next step was taken by the British.

In 1841, they appointed Dr. I.L. Tiarks, an astronomer, to study the problem. He finally took a map of the lake and a ruler. He placed the ruler across the lake at an exact NE to SW direction and then slowly moved it to the left across the map. He determined that the last point of shoreline touched by the ruler as it moved away from the lake would be the northwest point. Once the northwestern most point was established by Dr. Tiarks, he dropped a line straight south to the 49th parallel, thus creating the Northwest Angle of the United States. His decision was accepted by both sides, but it wasn't until 1872 that this point was finally announced as 29 23' 50.28 latitude and 95 08', 56.7 longtitude. The sometimes irregular boundary line between the Mouth of the Rainy River and the northwest point was worked out separately, thus deciding which islands would be American and which Canadian. In 1842, Daniel Webster and Lord Ashburton resolved the Minnesota-Ontario boundary from Lake Superior to Rainy Lake.

GARDEN ISLAND

In 1857, Simon Dawson, surveyor-explorer and Henry Hind, scientist, were assigned the task of finding the best all Canadian land water route to the Red River. Eastern Canadians and new immigrants from Europe were willing and anxious to emigrate west and the farmable lands of the Red River of the North were to be their first target area. Dawson had heard of the route used by the French explorers to the Red River via the warroad of the Indians. The voyageurs had not used this trail and its location was now only legend. Dawson did not know that the trail led through Minnesota and would therefore be useless to his government even if he did find it. He did know that the Indians were probably still aware of the trail and was quite certain they still used it. He was counting on them to show him the way.

All these plans went awry when Dawson stumbled onto an island in the Big Traverse area of Lake of the Woods - in the lower part of the Northwest Angle. It was no ordinary island. On it was a huge, cultivated garden, several acres in size! So far as he knew he was a thousand miles west of the nearest garden or farming of any kind. Dawson estimated that about five acres was planted in corn and another three acres in pumpkin, potatoes, and squash. Dawson and his crew helped themselves to samples from the garden and this was their mistake. The Indians who had been farming the island were unhappy with this presumptuous act and made it clear that they were not interested in exchanging gifts or friendship and that they definitely would not guide the party across the Indian shortcut to the Red River. Earl Chapin, in his booklet "The Angle of Incidents", quotes the chief as saying,

> "We wish to know what you are doing in our country. Who are these men? We have heard you have been gathering flowers, [Hind, the scientist, had for scientific classification]. What does that mean? You gathered corn in our garden and put it away. Did you never see corn before? Would not your people be satisfied if you just noted it down in your notebook? Or do you look at what the Indian has to come and settle here?"

The chief is quoted as continuing,

> "Give us no presents. We do not want them. We have hearts and love our lives and our country. We do not want the white man. When the white man comes he brings disease and sickness and our people perish. We do not wish to die. We wish to love and hold the land God has given to us and our fathers won. You must go by the old way [Winnipeg River] and not steal in by the window."

The lost portage sought by Dawson probably included two alternate routes: (1) up the west branch of the Warroad River with a portage to Hay Creek which empties into the Roseau River, and (2) up Reed River from Buffalo Bay with a portage to Mud Creek (Sprague River). John Tanner's description of the portage would indicate that he took the Reed River route:

"We then returned to the Lake of the Woods. From this lake, the Indians have a road to the Red River which White men never follow. This is by way of the muskeg carrying place. We went up Swamp River for several days [Probably Reed River], then we dragged our canoes across a swamp for one day. Then we put our canoes into a small stream called Begwionusk [cow parsley]; this we descended into a small lake."

Since the Warroad River route is not swampy and since the small lake referred to could only be Roseau Lake (now drained), it may be concluded that Tanner took the Reed River route to the Red River.

Dawson solved neither the secret of the lost portage nor the mystery of Garden Island. We don't know whether Dawson ever heard of the La Vérendryes, but if he had, and if he had searched the journals of Pierre La Vérendrye, he would have found the solution to the mystery of Garden Island in this insertion:

"I have induced two families of Indians, by earnest solicitations, to sow maize. I trust that the benefits they will derive therefrom will induce others to follow their example."

It is doubtful La Vérendrye ever dared hope his Chippewa friends and their descendants would be such successful and diligent farmers!

THE DAWSON TRAIL

Another Dawson (Dr. George M.)[1] was more successful. In 1873 he discovered the "lost portage". Historian John Parsons described it this way:

"From the lake they descended the Reed River, portaged seven Miles across a swamp and muskeg where the old canoe track was plainly visible, to the headwaters of the east Roseau [Mud Creek], and followed that stream down."

Dawson also had been commissioned to find an all-Canadian route to the upper Red River of the North where a small frontier colony was slowly but steadily growing. The "lost portage" proved to be on American soil, therefore, this phase of the exploration was in vain.

The Canadian government was determined to develop a route from Montreal to the Red River and Lake Winnipeg area because the isolated, fledging colony in the West had been aligning itself with the United States and with St. Paul and Minneapolis in particular. Although the route of travel from this area to southern Minnesota was far from easy, it was at least possible and far superior to the wilderness trail across Canada. In addition to the water route up the Minnesota and down the Red River the famous Ox Cart Trails were developed. The journey from Pembina, North Dakota, to St. Paul took 40 days, and it is said that the squeaking of the heavy wooden wheels of the oxen-drawn carts could be heard for a mile.

The Dominion Government was so determined to break through the wilderness that even a proposal to develop a system of canals from Lake Superior to Lake of the Woods was taken very seriously. At one point the administration decided to proceed with the actual construction and a large number of men were moved into the area. These became the first permanent settlers in the Fort Frances-International Falls region and along the south shore of Lake of the Woods. However, a change in administration in 1875 resulted in the plan being postponed and then dropped altogether.

[1] *Dr. George M. Dawson [1849-1901]; Director, Canadian Geological Society; mapped much of Canada; Dawson City of Yukon Territory was named for him.*

The canal at Fort Frances.

Final Report of the International Joint Commission

Red River Freighter   Courtesy Minnesota Historical Society

The ultimate solution was to use the established waterways from Lake Superior to Lake of the Woods - portages and all - and then carve a road through the wilderness west of the lake to the prairies. Thus, the "Dawson Trail" became a reality, starting where Harrison's Creek flows into the Angle Inlet and ending at Fort Garry (Winnipeg). The route from the Angle west was all by land, first by ox carts and later by stage lines. By 1874, the Dominion Government had spent a million and a quarter dollars (no mean sum for those days) on the Dawson route, and in that year more than 300 emigrants followed it to the Red River and Lake Winnipeg area.

THE TOWN OF "NOR'WEST ANGLE"

A century ago, the Northwest Angle boasted a Canadian settlement with a population of several hundred persons. It was actually located on American territory, on a triangle of land formed between Harrison's Creek and the inlet. The town sprang up and grew largely for two reasons: first, it was the end of the water route from the East and the start of the Dawson Road; and secondly, it was an important Hudson's Bay Company post. The activity also attracted many Indians to the area. Had the dream of a canal become a reality, chances are the village would have become a permanent settlement and the history and present-day development of Lake of the Woods would be quite different than we know it. The town's growth was cut short by the coming of the railroad to Kenora (and from there to Winnipeg). In 1877, Mary Fitzgibbons (in her book. "A Trip to Manitoba":) describes the community thus,

> "The Nor'west Angle is a little village at the northwest corner of the Lake of the Woods at the mouth of a name less river, or narrow arm of the lake. The banks on one side are high and wooded, the other side is high also but comparatively bare of shrubs and trees; while between them the river wanders hither and thither."

> "The company's house is a long, low, white building, with narrow windows and doors, neat fences and grass plots in front, and a kitchen garden showing signs of care and attention. The houses are one story log buildings and plastered with mud inside and out. There are also several birch wigwams, full of smoke and swarthy children, the owners squatting at their low doors."

In a few years the town of Nor'west Angle was gone, and today, only the historian and the archeologist can prove it ever existed.

CHAPTER V
The Wolseley Expedition

The year 1870 was of considerable significance to the history of the Lake of the Woods and the Canadian West. It was the year "law and order" arrived in the wilderness. Reports of revolts and lawlessness in the Red River area aroused sufficient concern on the part of the Dominion Government to send Lt. Col. John Garnet Wolseley with a contingent of 1200 men to that area via Lake of the Woods and Rat Portage. The small army included 350 regulars from the 60th Rifles or Royal Americans; the balance were "irregulars" including guides and boatsmen.

With so large a force, restoring order on the frontier would be no problem, but moving more than a thousand men with all their equipment across the Canadian wilderness was no small challenge. Because this was a military expedition they could not travel the usual and easier route along the Minnesota border, nor could they use the route most freight was taking in that day, namely via the Twin Cities up the Minnesota River to the Red River and then north to what is now the Winnipeg area. Although they traveled an established route, the size of the army made it necessary to literally carve a path through the Canadian wilderness. After a grueling three-month journey, they arrived at Rat Portage August 14, 1870. They had come all the way from Toronto in huge boats, each large enough to carry twenty men and all their personal equipment and provisions. The boats were portaged near Keewatin to the Winnipeg River. The remainder of the journey to Lake Winnipeg was comparatively easy.

The real significance of the expedition lay in the fact that law and order had come to the West. Colonel Wolseley had demonstrated that a sizeable military force could be moved across the wilderness whenever necessary and lawlessness would not be tolerated. The travel difficulties of the expedition were a dramatic demonstration of the need for improvement of the first Dawson route. Soon, thereafter, portages were improved, roads were built, and work was begun on a canal and locks which would make portaging around Koochiching Falls on the Rainy River unnecessary.

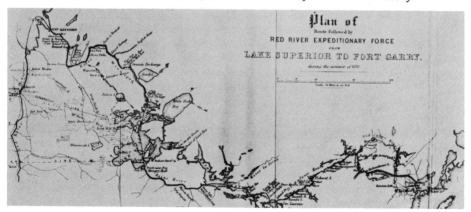

Plan of
Route followed by
RED RIVER EXPEDITIONARY FORCE
FROM
LAKE SUPERIOR TO FORT GARRY,
during the summer of 1870.

Route of expeditionary force, 1870.

Final Report of the International Joint Commission

CHAPTER VI
The Indian Treaty
Of 1873 (#3)

We have surmised how the Indian tribes fought one another for control of the Lake of the Woods. We have seen how this feuding continued during the days of discovery and exploration, lasting even through the rivalry of the Hudson's Bay Company and the North West Company. To be sure, the Indians resisted domination by the "foreigners", but far more blood was shed by Indian fighting Indian. The friendly feelings of the Chippewa for the French should not delude us into thinking they treated their fellow Indians in the same manner. They were not only ferocious fighters but showed no mercy for their opponents. Torture, scalping, and massacres - particularly of the Sioux - were not uncommon. Sioux Narrows was named for an ambush and massacre of the Indians of that name by the Chippewa. Part of the origin of the word "Chippewa" means "to pucker"; it is said this is what happened to the skins of their victims when they were tied to stakes "too close to the fire". The name given the Sioux by the Chippewa meant "roasters" and was associated with their practice of torturing victims at the stake![1]

The coming of Colonel Wolseley and his army of 1200 men in 1870 left little doubt in the minds of either the Indians or the whites who was in control of the country. Prior to that time, all attempts to work out a written agreement with the Indians as to which areas would be reserved for them and which would belong to the Dominion government were futile. We know that the government had long since assumed ownership of this entire area and had even parceled out much of it to the Hudson's Bay Company in 1870. The show of strength by Wolseley no doubt had a significant effect on the Indians and helped bring them to terms. However, even though there was no question the white man had taken over, it was deemed necessary that some legal agreement, binding on both parties, be worked out between the government and the Indians. The government wanted a clear and legal title to the lands. In return, they would pay the Indians sums of money and offer guarantees of peace, protection, education, etc. It was important to the conscience and image of the government (both at home and abroad) that the Indians enter into such an agreement of their own free will. At the very least, it had to appear that way.

The Indian must have realized that he really had little choice when faced with the overwhelming and industrially supported forces of the "invaders". About all he had going for him was the conscience of his adversary. We have seen how the Indians trusted the French. No doubt the treaties would have been more easily arranged if Canada had still been in the hands of France.

The Indian Treaty of 1873 (the third in Canada but the first in this area) was concerned with the general area from Lake Superior to Manitoba. It is believed that at that time there were about 14,000 Indians living in this region - which encompassed about 55,000 square miles.

Negotiating the treaty was no easy task. There were many independent tribes in the area and several chiefs - each of whom considered himself sovereign over his particular domain. It was very difficult, therefore, to strike an agreement among the Indians. Year after year the meetings between the government and the chiefs were

[1] Warren, William W., History of the Ojibways

postponed - until September, 1873. The conference finally took place on the North West Angle. Representing the government were: Alexander Morris, the Lieutenant Governor of Manitoba and the North West Territories; Lt. Colonel Provencher, representing the military; and S.J. Dawson, the explorer and now a member of parliament from Algoma. The official government delegation arrived on September 25th and took up headquarters at the Hudson's Bay Post; the Indians had already been in conference for several days[1] We find this interesting description in the diary of a soldier, probably one of Provencher's men:

> "Arrived Sept. 25. The governor of Manitoba arrived at 3:30. They mustered in Great force with squaws, papooses, etc. They marched around our camp headed by an old fellow in a soldier's coat and a Plug hat who looked like a broken-down admiral of the "Blue" with the jimjams. Their music consisted of four drums. They sang songs . . . The master of ceremonies wore a glaring red shirt with no sleeves, a plug hat, and white calico trousers. The clothing of most of the other braves was fancy but slight, consisting chiefly of nothing".

> "September 26. The Indians do not seem anxious to get to business. However, I do not blame them, for as long as they can make the affair last, the government is bound to supply them with food, etc. The way they gourmandized is simply alarming. Already two deaths from this cause has been reported."

> "October 1. The assembled braves during the pow wow would grunt incessantly, this to denote approbation, and when anything was mentioned about edibles, the grunting was terrible."

We often think of the historic Indian as a quiet man of few words. Actually he was often eloquent and quite poetic and when his words have been recorded by historians they have demonstrated both wisdom and beauty. Lest we leave the impression from the foregoing quotation that the Indians communicated only by grunts and gestures, let us look at some quotations taken from the archives of the Department of Indian Affairs at Ottawa. We who love the Lake of the Woods can understand the Indians' love for this country, but imagine the trauma they felt as they realized they were giving up all legal claim to their home and the home of their ancestors. Apart from certain reservations, they were about to become guests in their own land. Listen!

> Lt. Governor Morris: "Wood and water were the gifts of the Great Spirit, and were made alike for the White and the Red man."

> Pow-wa-sang: "What you say of the rivers and trees is quite true, but it was the Indians' country and not the White Man's."

> Ma-we-d-pe-nais: "The Great Spirit has planted us on this ground where we are - as you were where you came from. We think where we are is our property. He gave us rules to govern ourselves properly."

> Kee-ta-kay-pi-nais: "The sound of the rustling of gold is under my feet where I stand. We have a rich country. It is the Great Spirit who gave us this - where we stand upon is Indian property and belongs to them."

> Chief Sah-Katch-eway: "We are the first that were planted here; we would ask you to assist us with every kind of implement to use for our benefit, to enable us to perform our work, a little of everything and money. We would borrow your cattle, I will find thereon to feed them. The waters out of which you some times take food for yourselves we will lend you in return. If you give what I ask, the time may come when I will ask you to lend me one of your daughters and one of your sons to live with us, and in return I will lend you one of my daughters and one of

---

[1]Reports indicate that more than 1000 Indians may have been on hand.

my sons for you to teach what is good, and after they have learned, to teach us."
Chief Pa-pa-ska-gin: *"Listen to what I am going to say to you my brothers. We ask you not to reject some of our children who have gone out of our place; they are scattered all over. A good tasted meat has drawn them away and we wish to draw them all here to be contented with us. I would not like that anyone of my children should not eat meat with me."*
Chief Go-bay: *"We ask that the Indians may not have to pay their passage on the fire boats and the things that run swiftly by fire, but can go free and we must have the privilege to travel about the country where it is empty. We do not want anyone to mark out our reserves; we have already marked them out."*
Chief Canda-com-iga-wi-innie: *"You understand me now. I have taken your hand firmly and in friendship. I repeat twice that I have done so and with these promises you have made let the treaty be made. Let it be as you have promised for as long as the sun rises over our heads and as long as the water runs. One thing that deranges my kettle a little; in this land where food for our substance used to be plentiful, I perceive it has gone scarce. We wish that the river be left as it was found from the beginning - that nothing be broken."*

On October 3, 1873, when the treaty was finally consumated and about to be signed, Chiefs Mawe-do-pi-nais and Oaw-wa-sand spoke to Governor Morris thus as representatives of their people:

"Now we stand before you all. What has been done here today has been done openly before the Great Spirit and before the Nation. Never let anyone say it has been done secretly and in closing this Council I take off my glove and in giving you my hand I hold fast all the promises you have made and I hope they will last as long as the sun goes round and the water flows as you have said."

Governor Morris said in reply:

"I accept your hand and with it the lands and will keep all my promises, in the firm belief that the treaty now to be signed will bring the Red Man and the White Man together as friends forever."

The Treaty in its entirety as well as the orders establishing the negotiating commission is reproduced in the appendix. The concessions, cash settlements, and goods promised the Indians - as well as the pledges extracted in return - make especially interesting reading. For example, each chief was promised "an appropriate suit of clothes" every three years. Many Canadians living in the Lake of the Woods area can recall the blue serge suits which came to identify the chiefs. Although the treaty is not followed "to the letter", cash settlements are still made twice each year.

CHAPTER VII
Logging and Lumbering, A New Era

There is no hard line of demarcation between the fur trading era and the logging days. However the construction of the railroad to Rat Portage and from there west to Winnipeg in the early 1880's brought about the change in emphasis. Trapping remains an important part of the economy of the Lake of the Woods to this day, but the coming of the railroad created not only a need for timbers to construct the right of way but it also provided the means of transporting lumber out of the area and transporting people in who would soon build homes, churches, schools and places of business from the proud pines and spruce of the lake.

It is hard to equal the explorers for bravery or the voyageurs for color, but the loggers were a legend in their own right. Not as exciting perhaps as the authors of Paul Bunyan tales would have us to believe, but the drama of the logging camps and sawmills was one of the really great epics in the development of North America. Here in the Lake of the Woods district it had a special flavor because of the setting. Much of the logging took place along the shores and on the islands of the lake and along the hundreds of miles of rivers and streams which flow into Lake of the Woods. The enormous rafts of logs which were moved to the north end of the lake from all parts of the region must have been fantastic spectacles in themselves. Logs are still moved in rafts on the lake today, especially in the spring after winter cutting, but the volume is puny by comparison.

A PIONEER IN FINANCE

John Mather was one of the financial pioneers who made possible the opening up and development of the country. He was associated with the coming of both the railroad and the lumbering industry to the Rat Portage area. Mather, you will recall, was the man who was given the power to decide which of the communities at the north end of the lake was to be called "Keewatin Mills" and which would be called "Rat Portage". When the Bank of Ottawa was established in 1874, John Mather was elected to its Board of Directors. As his interests moved west he was instrumental in establishing a branch bank in Winnipeg and later in the two frontier villages which developed out of the Rat Portage trading posts. As an interesting sidelight, illustrative of the difficulties of transportation in those days, the safe for the Winnipeg bank had to come from Minneapolis north via the Red River. The journey took six weeks!

Mather had a contract with the Canadian Pacific Railroad to provide timbers for the ties and trestles. He began operating the first sawmill on the Lake of the Woods in 1880. His first contract was with Peter Campbell who was to "cut all the pine, spruce, and tamarack" on Tunnel Island, Rat Portage. Opening the mill was no easy task. Just getting the equipment from Minneapolis to the site of present day Kenora was a monumental ordeal. The heavy machinery had to be carried up the Minnesota River, down the Red River to Winnipeg, and across country by wagon and sleds to the North

West Angle (over the Dawson Trail). Barges were then constructed for the final leg of the journey to the north end of the lake.

Other mills soon sprang up in the Rat Portage and Keewatin Mills area and during the next decade logging operations spread over most of the Lake of the Woods. Timber was harvested from points as far away as the tributaries of the Rainy River (including the Vermillion, Rat Root, Little Fork, Big Fork, and Rapid Rivers on the Minnesota side and the Pune, Sturgeon, and Vallee Rivers on the Canadian side). All of these logs were transported to the mills at the north end of the lake.

Actually, the taking of timber from the Minnesota side was illegal. It is estimated that some eighty-five million feet of lumber were poached annually from the United States from 1890 to 1900! The U.S. Government was aware of these operations as early as 1878. Agents were sent out each year to warn the violators, but cutting resumed as soon as the authorities left the area. By 1900 most of the big timber had been harvested. The Morris Act of 1902 gave ownership of much of the Indian territories to the U.S. Government and in turn to the settlers. The diminished timber supply plus the fact that the United States Government took better care of the area when it was no longer "just Indian territory" brought an end to the timber poaching.

Courtesy Minnesota Historical Society

Horse power for a logging camp on the south shore of the Lake of the Woods at the turn of the century.

Loggers made good settlers, and with the coming of the railroad, the population of the Rat Portage - Keewatin Mills area grew rapidly. Prior to the coming of Col. Wolseley and his army in 1870, the north end of the lake had only a few trading posts and a handfull of white men. With the coming of "law and order" a few more hardy souls and adventurers were drawn to the area. Even some of the Colonel's men fell in love with the lake and stayed on or returned when the expedition to Winnipeg was over. By 1881, with the coming of the railroad and the start of the lumbering industry, the Rat Portage area had an official population of 4,564!

All of this time, the southern part of the lake and the Minnesota side remained undeveloped, with the exception of the village of Northwest Angle. There was extensive cutting in the southern part of the lake, but all logs were floated to the north end to be milled. The nearest railroad to the south was still eighty miles away, terminating at Tower, Minnesota, in the iron range area.

As we enjoy the heavily timbered islands and mainland of the lake today, it is hard to visualize the extent of the cutting. However, most of what we see is second growth or trees that were too young at the turn of the century to be harvested. The picture of the Regina Gold Mine on page 54 shows how thoroughly the land was denuded. Some virgin timber remains in testimony to the glory of the past. With a little exploration, the enormous stumps of giant white and Norway pine can still be found — but most have rotted away. The decayed remains of old logging camps also may still be discovered on Big Island,[1] The Alneau Peninsula and on the mainland.

---

[1] *As a point of interest: Big Island was once surveyed into townships; it was thought that someday it would be settled.*

CHAPTER VIII
Gold!

The logging operations were no sooner underway on Lake of the Woods than Gold fever set in. Although the exploration and the mining activities which followed included the whole lake, Kenora was the unquestioned center of the activity.

The exploration and excitement of discovery after discovery lasted more than a decade. Gold brought a fresh wave of migrants to the lake. Thousands of claims were registered. However, even though many mines were opened and successfully worked, the Lake of the Woods gold rush was forced to compete with one of the greatest strikes of all time anywhere: Alaska and the Yukon! Whereas the lake gave up its gold grudgingly through hard rock mining, the strike in the Northwest meant easier and far more productive operations through the pan and sluice box. Yet, thousands came and hundreds stayed to establish gold mining as an important and lasting facet of the Lake of the Woods economy. By the turn of the century (1900) the mining activities moved away from the lake to the north and east. The significance of the gold rush days is illustrated by the fact there were at one time thirty mines operating within twenty-two miles of Kenora. In 1894, E. Arnold, innkeeper of the Russell House in that city, listed the following mines and their distances from his establishment on the back of his advertising card:

"Distance from the Russell House, Rat Portage
to the Mines"

Mine	Distance	Mine	Distance
Winnipeg Consolidated	15 miles	Nickel Mine	3 miles
Sultana	6 miles	Esweiler	4 miles
Treasurer	10 miles	Rajah mines	6 miles
El Diver	10 miles	Keewatin	12 miles
Pine Portage	11 miles	Gold Hill	20 miles
King	9 miles	Dead Broke	20 miles
Black Jack	16 miles	Sultana Junior	6 miles
George Henan	13 miles	Eureka	9 miles
Home Stake	8 miles	Manitoba Consolidated	14 miles
Original Home Stake	22 miles	Minerva	9 miles
Bad Mines	9 miles	Gold Creek	7 miles
Woodchuck	16 miles	Three Friends	15 miles
Queen of Sheba	16 miles	Caribou	4 miles
Bullion	4 miles	Ben Harrison	3 miles
Three Ladies	9 miles	Argyle	10 miles

By the turn of the century, others could have been added to the list, including the Mikado, the Wendigo, Cedar Island, Cameron Island, and the Combine.

Mines located on Lake of the Woods farther than twenty-two miles from Kenora were not listed.

During the gold rush days, the heavy equipment could be transported only by rail or water; thus the lake was the scene of most activity. With the coming of roads and trucks, more profitable mines were established over a large area to the north and east. In more modern times, low gold prices caused the phasing out of all gold mining operations here as in many other parts of North America. However, the rising prices of

Regina mine, Whitefish Bay.   from the International Commission Final Report, 1917

the 1970's are changing the whole scene and gold is once again important to the economy of this part of Ontario.

Many of the original mines are again producing and Kenora is the hub of a gold mining area extending as far as two hundred miles to the north and east.

Recent discoveries to the north have been around Red Lake, Pickle Crow, Trout Lake, and Stanley Lake.

Rainy Lake was the setting for a less spectacular but still significant gold rush starting in July of 1893 with the discovery of gold on Little America Island by George W. Davis. Rainy Lake City sprang up on the shores of the lake about twelve miles east of International Falls. Between gold and logging, the community quickly grew into a bustling frontier town. It even had its own newspaper and an 1894 edition of the "Rainy Lake Journal" told of the start of the village of Koochiching, the forerunner of present day International Falls. In addition to the Little America mine, successful operations included the "Gold Harbor" and "Holman" mines.

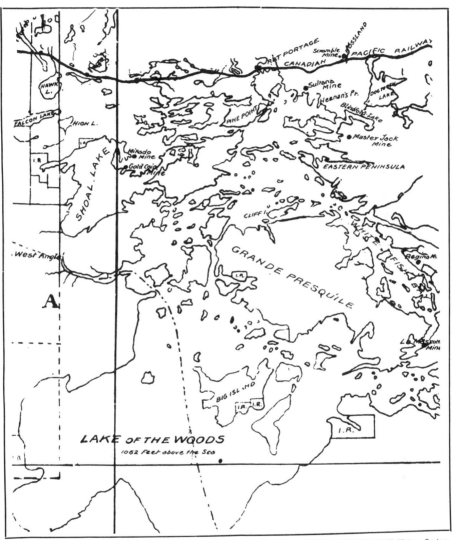

from the papers of George Bryce, 1897, "Lake of the Woods: It's History, Geology, Mining and Manufacturing.

19th century gold mines on Lake of the Woods.

CHAPTER IX
Canadian Northern Railway
Opens South End Of Lake

It is difficult to realize that there was virtually no development of the south shore of Lake of the Woods until this century. The discovery of iron ore in Minnesota resulted in the settling of the entire iron range area of the state during the 1800's, but the wilderness region of northern Minnesota remained unsettled until the coming of the Canadian Northern Railway. The railroad was also known as "the McKenzie and Mann" and is now part of the Canadian National System. In 1900, this railway joined Winnipeg with Port Arthur (Thunder Bay) and so far as the Lake of the Woods was concerned, resulted in the development of the communities of Fort Frances, International Falls, Rainy River, Baudette and Warroad. As the railroad traveled between the latter two villages it ran on Minnesota soil. Sawmills soon sprang up in those communities and along the south shore of the lake. The new activity along the Rainy River and the south shore did not significantly hinder the growth of the Kenora - Keewatin Mills area. The north end of the Lake already had a population of more than 10,000 people and was too involved in the gold rush and harvesting timber to worry much about competition from the southern part of the lake.

The American communities on the south shore remained separated from other Minnesota cities and villages until the coming of the Minnesota and International Railway in 1907 which joined International Falls with Brainerd and the Northern Pacific Railroad. In the same year the Duluth Winnipeg and Pacific connected International Falls with Duluth and the Iron Range cities in between.

The stage was then set for the growth and development of the south shore of the Lake of the Woods.

Steam locomotive on display at Rainy River, Ontario.

CHAPTER X
The Steamboat Era

During the latter part of the nineteenth century and the first part of this century, scores of steamboats cruised the waters of the Lake of the Woods. Kenora was home port for the largest number of vessels, but others steamed out of Warroad, Baudette, and the Rainy Lake area. They were of all shapes, sizes, and designs.

The first steamboat of importance was named "The Lady of the Lake" and sailed out of Rat Portage. It was 115 feet in length and was originally driven by side paddle wheels; later it was converted into a "sternwheeler". By the time the vessel was dismantled in 1880, steamboats had become the principal means of transporting passengers, lumber, and freight between Rat Portage, the North West Angle, Fort Frances and the several American ports - including those along Rainy River.

The negotiation of the Treaty of 1873 between the Indian tribes of the area and Her Majesty's Government considered (but apparently ignored) the Indians' request for free transportation on these "fire boats and the things which run swiftly by fire".

The "Agwinde" and the "Itasca" on the Rainy River.   Courtesy Minnesota Historical Society

Every ship had an appropriate name and the Kenora "Centennial Review", published in 1936, included a list of steamboats with such names as "The Swallow," "The Shamrock", "Edna Bridges", "Daisy Moore", "the Keenora", "Agwinde", "Monarch", "Empress", "D.L. Mather", "City of Alberton", "Verbena", and "Sir William Van Horne".

Early vessels out of Warroad included the "Na Ma Puk". In fact, the first issue of the Warroad "Plaindealer" (May 11, 1899) featured an article which described the vessel as being within two weeks of completion.

We do not know how many steamboats claimed Fort Frances or International Falls as "home port", but it is estimated that in the year 1890 there were twenty-one steam powered boats sailing between these "twin cities" and Rat Portage.

And so, just as the birchbark canoe dominated the scene from the days before the coming of the White Man through the time of the voyageurs, the black smoke of the steamboat characterized the new era of lake transportion before and after the turn of the century.

With the coming of the gasoline engine, the steamboats were replaced by inboard power launches and then the outboard motor. Some of the larger work boats of today are diesel powered and "inboard - outboards" are popular on pleasurecrafts. Sleek, cedar strip Peterboroughs added a beauty of their own to the lake scene during the first half of this century and seemed a fitting compromise between the wilderness and the new age of power. Because of the cost and nuisance of the upkeep of wood construction, these boats have now been largely replaced by aluminum and fiberglass - neither of which seem in harmony with our wilderness paradise.

CHAPTER XI
The Economics
Of The Lake

TOURISM

Although statistics are not available, there is a concensus that tourism is the most significant industry in the area today. This has been true since well before World War II, where the development of highways and roads opened the lake to property ownership and resorts. The Ministry of Transportation and Communications for Ontario provided the following information regarding the original construction of the provincial road system in the Lake region:

From Kenora easterly to the junction with Highway 71 [to Fort Frances] - 1930-31.

From Kenora westerly to the Ontario-Manitoba border - 1932 [official opening].

From Nestor Falls to Fort Frances - 1932-33.

From Nestor Falls to Kenora - 1933-35 [opened officially in 1936].

Northwest Angle - The Ontario-Minnesota Pulp and Paper Company has had a winter "haul road" since about 1953 out of East Braintree [Highway 12] in the Province of Manitoba.

On the Minnesota side of the border, the state highway department has no record of when the trails first became gravel roads. The Department does report, however, that bituminous plant mix surfacing first reached Warroad in 1937, International Falls in 1940, and Baudette in 1948.

There has been a noticeable change in the American tourists seen on the Lake since the road to Kenora was opened in 1935. When the Lake of the Woods was the "end of the road", those who came were mostly fishermen and hunters in search of outdoor adventure. These more adventuresome types now travel much farther north, not only to the end of the road but by air even beyond the Arctic Circle. Today, the whole family finds recreation in the Lake of the Woods area. Most of the resorts are as modern as those found in "the states", yet the wilderness remains. We have the best of both worlds.

At this writing, 1975, a gravel road is under construction from Highway 71 north of Nestor Falls to the Indian Reserve on Sabaskong Bay. It may be continued to Turtle Lake. The road is being built on Indian owned land with Ojibway tribal funds.

Further encroachment on the wilderness will come slowly in as much as no new resorts or camps can be opened on Crown Land. Furthermore, islands still owned by the government (and that means nearly all of those still undeveloped) may no longer be purchased.

HUNTING, SPORT FISHING, AND TRAPPING

Excellent fishing remains the chief attraction. The Lake of the Woods is known far and wide as one of the top lakes on the continent for walleyes and northern pike.

Author with northern taken in early June.

Steve Clabots with mallards taken before breakfast while paddling through heavy rice.

Leland Standiford didn't mind coming all the way from Georgia to catch this slab size crappie.

The author with a mixed bag possession limit of ducks.

[from left to right] The author, Harold Wolfe, and Steve White with possession limits of mallards and bluebills [and "Sam" the lab retriever]

The author with a winter walleye.

Happy hunter, Don Hester, with 262 pound Alneau Peninsula buck.

Bruce Lund with Ring Bill ducks which took a fancy to this secluded bay. Decoys in background.

Mixed bag of 8 point buck and Sabaskong Bay ducks makes a smile come easy for Jerry Hayenga.

Nearly every variety of fresh water fish found in this part of the world swims in its waters. Sport fish other than pike include lake trout, muskellunge, small mouth bass, and crappie. The record fish, however, is a 238 pound sturgeon!

Final Report of the International Joint Commission

As good as hunting is today in the Lake of the Woods area, big game probably came easier for this turn-of-the-century hunting party.

Hunting, another major attraction, includes such big game as moose, bear, and white tail deer (moose, however, can be hunted on the Canadian part of the Lake by residents only). Hundreds of thousands of ducks nest on the Lake every spring and the migration from farther north is a fall spectacle. Geese visit mostly the western part of the lake on their way south. Partridges (ruffed grouse) abound on the shores and sharptails can be found in the open field areas south of the lake and on a few of the larger islands. There are some spruce hens, but they are comparatively rare.

Not everyone comes to fish and hunt; many enjoy camping, boating, canoeing, or just drinking in the wilderness scenery of the Lake of the Woods with its clean water and 14,000 wooded islands.

The timber wolf is well established in the Lake of the Woods area and they are sometimes seen cutting across the winter ice. Other predators such as the lynx and fox are common. The fur bearing animals which originally drew the early explorers and voyageurs to the area are still with us, including beaver, mink, muskrat, martin, fisher, weasel, and otter. Trapping continues to help support the economy of the lake area, but is largely an income supplement. Raccoon, skunk, rabbits, squirrels, and miscellaneous rodents are among the smaller inhabitants. If you watch carefully you may even see a tiny hopping rodent known as the kangaroo mouse.

An elk herd was started many years ago on the Minnesota side of the border. It has seldom exceeded a few dozen in number over the years. Caribou once migrated as far south as the Lake of the Woods in early spring. Even now we hear stories of sightings of small bands at the north end of the Lake. The Ontario Department of Land and Forests advises that "It has been confirmed that three caribou were seen in 1973 near Ingolf - about ten miles north of Shoal Lake". The normal southern extent of their migration is Lake Umfreville, forty-five miles northwest of Kenora.

At the turn of the century, Woodland Caribou were actually hunted in Minnesota. Herds were fairly common north of Red Lake and along the north shore of Lake Superior.

In prehistoric times the buffalo came as far east as the Lake. Buffalo wallows[1] remain as a testimony to the visits of this great animal in the Buffalo Point area.

TIMBER AND WOOD PRODUCTS

In Chapter XII, entitled "Communities of the Lake", we will find that the economy of virtually every village is dependent to a great degree on logging and/or the manufacture of lumber, paper and wood products. In fact, most of the communities are located where they are because sawmills were originally built at those sites. The first mills were at the north end of the Lake because that is where the railroad was first constructed (1881). The forests of the south shore and of northern Minnesota fed the mills at Rat Portage until 1890 when the coming of the railroad made sawmills possible from Rainy Lake to Warroad.

In spite of nearly a century of logging, the Lake of the Woods remains heavily timbered with its beauty relatively unmarred. Although a good deal of the forests we see today are second growth, some virgin timber still remains. The Canadian government has wisely regulated cutting in this century. The Ontario Ministry of Natural Resources advises that -

> No cutting is allowed at distances of less than 400 feet to 600 feet on shoreline reserves.
> No cutting is allowed in Indian reserves except by Indians.
> No cutting is allowed on islands which are less than 200 acres; on certain islands no cutting is allowed regardless of size, i.e. Bigsby Island.
> The species that may be cut are set out in the Management Plan for the Alneau Management Unit, i.e. volumes that may be cut are regulated by the allowable cut for that species.

The cutting of trees in wilderness areas is always controversial; however, the Dominion Government has tried to keep the harvesting of timber from spoiling the environment. Most logging takes place during the winter, and it is usually very difficult to identify these logging sites during the summer months. Not only is cutting prohibited in view of the lake, but the access trails are usually hidden in deep bays and are kept as narrow as possible. It should also be pointed out that the cutting of trees is highly beneficial to wildlife. Stands of virgin timber usually form an umbrella which prevents the sunshine from filtering down to the undergrowth which is the actual source of food for both birds and animals. With the heavy demand for wood products and paper in particular, we can expect more logging in the future than in recent decades - not less. However, if the government continues to vigorously enforce its cutting regulations, it may just be that we, and the wild life, can have the best of both worlds.

There is some evidence that Indians purposely burned large tracts of forest land so that the berry crops would improve and animal life would have better browse. Father Alneau wrote of huge fires set by Indians and encountered by him as he traveled west to Fort St. Charles.

---

[1]A buffalo wallow is usually a huge rock around which the animals walked while rubbing their itchy hides against the hard surface. The track was often worn several feet deep and the irregular surface of the rock was polished smooth in places.

courtesy Boise Cascade Co., International Falls

Logging operations in the Lake of the Woods area today.

MINERALS

In Chapter Eight we saw how the gold rush of the 1890's brought thousands to the Lake of the Woods area, and even though the strike lost much of its impact because of the far greater finds at that time in Alaska and the Yukon, the discovery of gold did have a lasting effect on the Lake of the Woods area. Kenora has remained the center of mining activity since the beginning and now services a 200 mile area to the north and east. New discoveries coupled with the escalating price of gold promise a significant increase in mining activity, but hopefully not on the lake itself! Mining activities are often far less compatable with wilderness areas than logging operations.

Other minerals found in the Lake of the Woods area (largely to the north and east) include copper, nickle, iron, and manganese. To what extent they may ever be mined commercially is, of course, speculation.

COMMERCIAL FISHING

Fish were a major source of food for the Indian down through the centuries. When La Verendrye and his men built Fort St. Charles, they established a winter fishing camp (probably at the mouth of the Grassy River), so we know that they, too, were dependent on the fish of the lake for survival. When the Treaty of 1873 was negotiated between Her Majesties government and the Indians of the area, the chiefs expressed a concern that the fish supply was being depleted by the white man. Just as soon as the railroad made it possible to ship fish to eastern markets, netting fish for money began in earnest. Commercial fishing was identifiable as an industry on Lake of the Woods by 1885 when commercial pound nets were used for the first time. By 1896, more than 300 pound nets were in use in Minnesota and Ontario waters. The Minnesota Legislature first established commercial fishing regulations for Lake of the Woods in 1895. Commercial fishing has continued both in Canadian and United States waters to the present. At the turn of the century the usual price for northern pike was three cents a pound and four cents for walleyes. One early transaction involved seven sturgeon (the smallest of which was forty pounds) traded for one cotton shirt. In this century, there has been the ever increasing pressure of sports fishing and today - as if the fish didn't have trouble enough already with nets, guides, and irresistible lures of all descriptions - we now have electronic devices to indicate temperature, depth, and the very location of the fish themselves! Yet, through it all, fishing has remained excellent. Not only are limit catches of all varieties produced consistently, but trophy size fish are caught in considerable numbers every year. Whitefish Bay continues to produce some of the largest lake trout caught anywhere and Sabaskong Bay and the North West Angle area yield muskies of record class. For many years the world record muskellunge was credited to the Lake of the Woods and national fishing contests have historically had heavy contributions from the Lake.

How can a lake have all this fishing pressure for nearly a century and remain among the best walleye, muskie, and northern pike lakes of the continent? The answer lies in the ideal spawning conditions provided by its 65,000 mile shoreline (longer than Lake Superior) and its 1980 square miles of water. The entire Lake of the Woods watershed actually includes about 27,000 square miles and the hundreds of rivers and streams which drain this watershed not only have their share of fish but provide additional spawning grounds.

Lake of the Woods sturgeon.

from the International Joint Commission Final Report, 1917

Table 1. Fish species reported in Lake of the Woods in studies made by Evermann and Latimer [1910], Carlander [1942], and Muth and Smith [1974].[1]

Petromyzontidae
  Silver lamprey, *Ichthyomyzon unicuspis* Hubbs and Trautman

Acipenseridae
  Lake sturgeon, *Acipenser fulvescens* Rafinesque

Hiodontidae
  Mooneye, *Hiodon tergisus* LeSueur
  Goldeye, *Hiodon alosoides* (Rafinesque)

Salmonidae
  Tullibee, *Coregonus artedii* LeSueur
  Lake whitefish, *Coregonus clupeaformis* (Mitchill)
  Lake trout, *Salvelinus namaycush* (Walbaum)

Esocidae
  Northern pike, *Esox lucius* Linnaeus
  Muskellunge, *Esox masquinongy* Mitchill

Catostomidae
  Quillback, *Carpiodes cyprinus* (LeSueur)
  White sucker, *Catostomus commersoni* (Lacepede)
  Longnose sucker, *Catostomus catostomus* (Forster)
  Silver redhorse, *Moxostoma anisurum* (Rafinesque)
  Shorthead redhorse, *Moxostoma macrolepidotum* (LeSueur)
  Northern hog sucker, *Hypentelium nigricans* (LeSueur)

Cyprinidae
  Emerald shiner, *Notropis atherinoides* Rafinesque
  Spottail shiner, *Notropis hudsonius* (Clinton)
  Common shiner, *Notropis cornutus* (Mitchill)
  Redfin shiner, *Notropis umbratilis* (Girard)
  River shiner, *Notropis blennius* (Girard)
  Rosyface shiner, *Notropis rubellus* (Agassiz)
  Blacknose shiner, *Notropis heterolepis* Eigenmann and Eigenmann
  Golden shiner, *Notomigonus crysoleucas* (Mitchill)

Ictaluridae
  Black bullhead, *Ictalurus melas* (Rafinesque)
  Tadpole madtom, *Noturus gyrinus* (Mitchill)

Percopsidae
  Trout-perch, *Percopsis omiscomaycus* (Walbaum)

Gadidae
  Burbot, *Lota lota* (Linnaeus)

Gasterostidae
  Ninespine stickleback, *Pungitius pungitius* (Linnaeus)

Centrarchidae
  Rockbass, *Ambloplites rupestris* (Rafinesque)
  Black crappie, *Pomoxis nigromaculatus* (LeSueur)
  Smallmouth bass, *Micropterus dolomieui* Lacepede

Percidae
  Iowa darter, *Etheostoma exile* (Girard)
  Johnny darter, *Etheostoma nigrum* Rafinesque
  River darter, *Percina shumardi* (Girard)
  Logperch, *Percina caprodes* (Rafinesque)
  Yellow perch, *Perca flavescens* (Mitchill)
  Sauger, *Stizostedion canadense* (Smith)
  Walleye, *Stizostedion vitreum vitreum* (Mitchill)

Cottidae
  Mottled sculpin, *Cottus bairdi* Girard

The author has also caught sunfish in Lake of the Woods. However, they were quite small and apparently stunted.

[1] *Muth and Smith, The burbot Fishery in Lake of the Woods, U of M, 1974.*

Although the total number of fish taken over the years has increased slightly the number of walleyes and northern pike taken by commercial fishing has diminished considerably in recent times. Much of the take is now rough fish.

Commercial fishing has had a profound effect on the fish population of the lake. We know from records kept on the Minnesota side of Lake of the Woods that there has been a dramatic change in the fish population over the years. Before the turn of the century, sturgeon made up over one-half of the commercial catch and Lake of the Woods was one of the continent's principal sources of this giant remnant of the glacial age. By 1920, they were all but extinct for commercial purposes. The whitefish population on Minnesota waters was so depleted by the late 1930's that it had no further commercial value. More restrictive legislation was adopted by the Minnesota legislature in 1941 setting size limits for sauger, walleye, northern pike, and whitefish. The taking of sturgeon, muskellunge, bass, and crappies by commercial means was outlawed altogether. Commercial fishermen were limited to the use of no more than six pound nets, 10 fyke nets, or 4,000 feet of gill nets. Both fishermen and fishermen's helpers were required to be licensed. The commercial fishing opening was set for June 1 of each year and certain parts of the lake were placed off limits so as to not conflict with sport fishing.

Most commercial fishing on Lake of the Woods is done as a family business with the "know how" passed along from generation to generation.

Fishing gear is closely regulated. Gill nets, pound nets, trap nets, and fyke nets are all legal, but each must meet specific criteria. For example gill nets in Minnesota waters must have a minimum size of four inches stretched mesh and must not exceed a depth of 30 meshes. Incidentally, gill nets are the most common because they are the easiest to stake out and retrieve and simply depend on the fish swimming into the net and becoming entangled. Also, they can be easily used under the ice. The disadvantage is that the unwanted fish can seldom be released without gill damage and the nets must be tended regularly or the fish will die or deteriorate in quality.

Pound nets are the second most often used; they are hung on stakes and depend on fish following a lead net into a funnel-shaped heart and then into a pot or crib from which they cannot escape.

Trap nets are very much like pound nets but are designed for special locations such as channels.

Fyke nets are hoop or barrel nets; they are awkward to handle but may also be used for winter fishing under the ice. These last three types of nets are all more difficult to handle than gill nets and require at least two men to stake them out and tend them. Their advantage is that fish keep better and the unwanted fish can be returned unharmed.

Commercial trawlers were used on Big Traverse in 1961 and 1962 and from 1968 to 1970 on an experimental basis. They are not legal at this writing.

Figure 1 shows the Minnesota commercial catch from the start of record keeping in 1888 to 1970 both in terms of millions of pounds and percent of each species. The sharp increase in the five year period from 1960-1964 was probably the result of good burbot and tulibee populations and the experimental use of trawlers, a technique which was particularly effective in the harvesting of these two varieties.

The Booth Fisheries, located at Warroad and long associated with the history of the Lake are now owned by the Morey Fish Company of Motley, Minnesota. Although a high demand continues for walleye and northern pike, the market for rough fish has dropped as many mink ranches have been forced to close because of foreign competition.

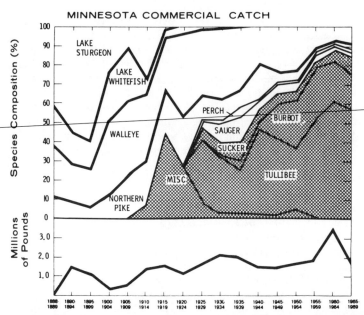

Figure 1. Minnesota commercial fisheries catches from Lake of the Woods averaged over 5-year intervals expressed as percentage species composition and pounds harvested.

Table 2. Commercial harvest of fish from Minnesota waters of Lake of the Woods from 1930 to 1972, expressed as pounds

Year	Species						
	Walleye	Sauger	Perch	Tullibee	Sucker	Northern pike	Burbot
1930	768,225	73,602	54,721	903,023	125,102	227,628	—
1931	954,818	218,657	55,883	435,225	126,000	168,352	—
1932	625,536	215,898	36,698	1,296,467	117,718	150,564	45
1933	670,600	242,500	40,000	293,300	168,300	260,200	63,974
1934	891,600	282,500	43,700	155,500	120,000	349,500	91,344
1935	1,020,700	346,500	77,800	131,600	183,300	246,500	175,480
1936	846,600	391,400	156,000	103,100	230,600	197,300	178,649
1937	636,400	415,000	218,700	223,300	183,600	163,400	70,965
1938	362,600	87,900	53,600	878,120	180,300	137,900	20,602
1939	332,225	68,987	50,179	910,508	161,666	146,900	46,746
1940	520,790	82,072	41,259	1,184,851	100,297	168,435	42,037
1941	643,209	69,625	16,688	471,513	98,138	126,417	49,082
1942	420,547	55,761	11,965	533,920	118,814	86,150	74,293
1943	343,828	56,850	12,552	549,592	151,566	105,319	51,154
1944	346,183	33,458	8,703	689,175	106,033	104,921	39,634
1945	367,538	37,965	6,456	238,212	109,715	91,229	122,839
1946	345,714	44,798	17,508	419,600	83,687	84,802	203,484
1947	299,855	77,988	27,517	519,480	100,000	66,040	247,807
1948	303,090	63,165	24,498	1,062,913	68,800	73,899	539,985
1949	419,154	116,880	21,720	771,604	71,383	86,747	578,767
1950	353,671	107,725	14,770	763,314	84,709	73,485	436,991
1951	257,681	73,912	11,595	387,866	73,447	80,580	425,753
1952	366,487	42,250	21,624	712,666	76,060	76,919	540,753
1953	480,835	66,335	26,148	438,285	95,582	104,038	296,293
1954	326,307	63,594	12,792	314,474	66,776	104,638	452,690
1955	233,639	69,179	20,055	591,516	63,661	52,969	449,711
1956	245,472	109,579	19,775	644,165	38,152	54,768	496,342
1957	204,531	63,598	12,354	664,353	33,298	81,551	564,234
1958	170,278	37,915	21,417	1,767,496	117,652	59,654	356,024
1959	220,345	36,567	20,871	1,252,860	58,568	47,305	650,092
1960	429,802	59,929	17,192	1,649,031	69,787	49,090	755,106
1961	324,038	117,844	25,614	2,160,260	200,011	58,376	882,561
1962	165,857	144,771	28,271	2,660,669	167,715	60,254	767,830
1963	224,932	84,356	19,505	2,029,785	247,813	74,299	571,675
1964	217,030	68,472	11,554	2,203,501	203,479	76,066	594,582
1965	140,888	42,826	8,414	843,684	282,427	59,926	351,859
1966	305,218	27,286	22,762	921,827	195,814	64,028	285,530
1967	138,180	25,645	28,069	862,810	185,650	33,846	467,288
1968	107,344	16,847	36,053	1,224,334	106,332	51,480	365,625
1969	81,554	13,054	21,343	1,139,707	65,195	66,932	253,516
1970	102,756	17,421	12,703	758,300	111,238	57,816	175,841
1971	129,435	16,638	5,619	618,309	89,467	63,413	262,171
1972	286,922	13,006	10,470	794,715	151,590	66,551	161,478

Muth & Smith, The Burbot Fishery in Lake of the Woods, U of M, 1974

No one can argue that commercial fishing helps sports fishing (unless only rough fish are netted), but just how much it hurts on a body of water such as the Lake of the Woods is still debatable.

WILD RICE

Wild Rice is an exotic food. This is partly so because of its unique flavor and uses and partly because it is relatively rare. Minnesota and Ontario have almost a natural monoply on the grain. It really isn't a rice at all, but has its own separate identity. Some say it is nothing more than "a valuable weed". Nevertheless, it has been a very expensive food over the years because of the uncertain crop conditions and the difficulty in harvesting it by boat. Prices have been reduced in the 1970's because for the first time it is now being grown successfully, commercially, in Minnesota. A major breakthrough occurred when a "non-shattering" variety was developed with the help of the University of Minnesota. True wild rice can not be grown very easily commercially because it is so difficult to harvest. A few grains ripen at a time in the head of the plant and these must be dislodged by pulling the plants over the boat and beating them with a stick - just as the Indians had done for hundreds of years. Those kernels not harvested when they become ripe, simply drop off and are lost. The process has to be repeated over several days as additional grains ripen. The "non-shattering" variety is a type where nearly all the grains remain in the head until they are all ripe and can, therefore, be harvested at one time by machine. Non-shattering rice is controversial, however, and many commercial growers have deserted it for more natural varieties. In addition to problems of quality and quantity this variety has proven more vulnerable to weather, disease, etc. In Minnesota, the commercial growers have developed patties which can be drained at planting and harvest time, so that machines can easily be used.

Wild rice will probably continue to be harvested in its natural state for many years, but it will never again be as profitable. Wild rice has not been a major factor in the economy of the Lake of the Woods in this century but it has been an important income supplement. The crop is unpredictable and highly dependent on water levels in the spring of the year. Relatively low water is needed for the seed to germinate. In 1972, a relatively good year, it was estimated that the Lake of the Woods contained about 7000 acres of wild rice.

Although the relative economic value today is quite small compared to tourism, timber, and mining, it should be remembered that for centuries, wild rice was of enormous importance to the survival of the Indian people.

Wild rice is also important to the water fowl of the Lake, and is responsible for the large populations of the so-called "puddle ducks" or "dabblers" such as mallards and wood ducks. Wild rice is not important to the diets of diving ducks, with the exception of ring bills. If this exotic food is some day harvested entirely in commercial paddies, the ducks won't mind a bit!

CHAPTER XII
Communities Of The Lake

BAUDETTE

Because the community is located at the confluence of the Baudette and Rainy Rivers and is so close to the Lake of the Woods, it was probably an Indian village site from time to time over the centuries. The first white man to see the river banks on which Baudette grew, was no doubt Jacques De Noyon, the discoverer of Lake of the Woods. We know that he came to the Lake via the Rainy River route. The La Verendryes, De la Nove, the voyageurs, and many others also passed this way before the white man's village was built here.

When the railroad came to the south end of the Lake in 1901, sawmills sprang up all the way from Rainy Lake to Warroad and Baudette was born as another "lumber town". It was not incorporated as a village until 1906. Today it is a thriving community of more than 1600 population and serves as the county seat of Lake of the Woods County (Minnesota's youngest and most sparsely settled county).

Baudette is still served by the Canadian National Railway, which enters the United States at this point and re-enters Canada at Warroad. The railroad has been servicing the area since 1890 - before Baudette was incorporated as a village.

The village was almost entirely destroyed by fire in 1910. It is difficult today to realize what a threat forest fires were to the early villages located in the heavily timbered areas of North America. Actually, dozens of these towns and hundreds of farm buildings were "wiped out" by raging fires early in this century. The death toll was often heavy. Devastating fires swept through thousands of acres of Lake of the Woods timber in 1734, 1803-04, 1894, and 1910.

As a gateway to the south end of the Lake of the Woods, Baudette has become a tourist center. However, the economy of the village is also dependent on Rowell Laboratories, the U.S. Air Force Radar Station, Agriculture, and logging.

The Rowell Laboratories were founded in 1929 by T.H. Rowell, a pharmacist. Rowell's father was a commercial fisherman and Ted was familiar with the Lake's large population of burbot![1] He was aware that it was a fresh water cousin of the ocean codfish. Rowell learned to extract the vitamin rich oil from the large fish livers and found a national market for his product. In those days the children of the northern climates of the world were fortified against colds by generous doses of cod liver oil (a horrible tasting liquid which usually required a "chaser" of jelly or some other sweet, but actually a good source of Vitamins A & D). With the coming of World War II the national supply dried up and the burbot of the Lake of the Woods became the source of the "missing" vitamins. Today, the liver extract is relatively a small part of the business, as Rowell Laboratories manufactures a great variety of pharmaceutical products for world wide distribution. The company specializes in preparations for clinics and University hospitals. It is not a little suprising to find such an industry on the

---

[1] A rough fish sometimes called eel-pout lawyer or ling Cod and the sole surviving fresh water species of the Codfish family.

very edge of the wilderness. It's success is a real tribute to the Rowell family and the nearly 100 employees who have contributed to its growth.

Ted Rowell, Sr., the founder of the company, was also chairman of the committee that worked long and tirelessly for the construction of the International Bridge across the Rainy River - joining the twin cities of Baudette, Minnesota, and Rainy River, Ontario. The bridge was constructed in 1960 and was made possible by federal support resulting from legislation introduced by U.S. Senator Edward J. Thye (R. - Minn.) in 1958.

Prior to 1960 a ferry service was operated during the open water seasons and cars crossed on the ice in winter.

Agriculture, another bulwark of the Baudette economy, contributes about one and a half million dollars annually to that economy through the sale of farm products. The soil is quite fertile and crops such as wheat, oats, barley, rye, flax, red and sweet clover seed, timothy seed, and potatoes for seed have been found suitable to the cool climate and relatively short growing season.

Timber products contribute another three quarter million dollars annually to the Baudette economy. Two lumber and wood products plants are located in nearby Williams. Although the village of Williams is not on the Lake, it is the gateway to Zippel Bay State Park[1] which is on the south shore of the Lake of the Woods.

Baudette - 4th of July Parade down 2nd street, 1912.   Courtesy Minnesota Historical Society

The United States Air Force Radar Station located just south of the city has contributed much to the business community since it was established in 1959. Since the expansion of the facility in 1969 when it became a BUIC III site, the base has employed about 250 military personnel.

A tool and die shop which also specializes in metal stampings (the Wabanica Products Company) is also located in Baudette.

Originally, a separate village known as "Spooner", was located across the Baudette River. It was incorporated as part of the village of Baudette in 1954. It was in Spooner that the great Shevin - Mathieu Mill was established in 1905. Here 60 million board feet of lumber was processed annually and 350 men were employed on a double shift. The mill was destroyed by fire in 1921.

FORT FRANCES

Although the community is located approximately eighty miles up Rainy River from the Lake of the Woods, the history of Fort Frances is closely entwined with that of the Lake. Strategically located on the water route from the East at the west end of Rainy Lake, it became a natural stopping place for explorers, voyageurs, fur traders.

The Zippel family were pioneers in commercial fishing on the Lake.

missionaries and early settlers. The coming of roads and the construction of the international bridge (1912) made it the major port of entry between Minnesota and Ontario.

Jacques de Noyon, the first white man to discover the Lake of the Woods, headquartered in this area. La Verendrye's first fort (St. Pierre) was erected by his nephew (La Jemeraye) in the vicinity of what is now Pither's Point in 1731.

A missionary once described Rainy Lake as a gathering place of -

> *Generally from two to five thousand Indians in the immediate vicinity of the company's fort; and during a part of the year, their numbers may be estimated at not less than 2000. Rainy Lake is one of the principal places in the country for holding the Great Medicine Feasts.*

"The Monarch", owned by Mosher Brothers and docked at Fort Frances. Old Hudson's Bay buildings are in the background.

In 1793 the Northwest Trading Company built a compound at Fort Frances below the falls and named it Fort Lac La Pluie. The very next year Duncan McGillvray visited the fort and described what was perhaps the first labor dispute in the West. It had to do with a strike by some men of one of the "fur brigades" against the trading company.

> *A few discontented persons in their band, wishing to do as much mischief as possible, assembled their companions together several times on the voyage outward and presented to them how much their interest suffered by the passing obedience to the will of their masters, when their ability to the company might ensure them not only of better treatment, but of many other conditions which they would prescribe with Spirit and Resolution.*
>
> *. . . They all declared with one voice that unless their wages would be augmented, and several other conditions equally unreasonable, granted them, they would immediately set off to Montreal . . . yet, a timidity was observed in*

their behavior which proved very fortunate for their masters, who took good advantage of them and before night prevailed on a few of the most timid to return to their duty, and the rest being ashamed to abandon their companions, soon followed the example . . . a few of the most resolute were obstinate enough to hold out . . . and were therefore sent to Montreal in disgrace.

In 1825, following the merger of the Northwest Trading Company with the Hudson's Bay Company, the governor of the new conglamorate, George Simpson, visited the fort with his bride, Frances Ramsey Simpson. The result was the renaming of the fort in honor of the young Mrs. Simpson, hence: Fort Frances.

The "fort" burned in 1874 but was restored and served as a trading post until 1897 or 1898. About that time it ceased to be a fur trading center and was used only as a retail outlet until it was destroyed again by fire in 1903, and never replaced.

Following the fur trading era, lumbering became the chief industry. Wood and wood products remain the chief factor in the community's economy. Initially, the logs were floated to Rat Portage at the north end of the Lake of the Woods. The coming of the Canadian Northern Railroad in 1902 resulted in sawmills from Rainy Lake all the way down the river and along the south shore of the Lake of the Woods as far as Warroad. Actually, a few mills were opened on Rainy River as early as 1890.

Courtesy Minnesota Historical Society

Koochiching Rapids from the Canadian side.

The dam at Koochiching Falls was built over a five year period from 1905-1910. Its completion provided the opportunity for power and the coming of the paper industry. The Fort Frances Paper Mill was in operation by 1914. The original ownership was forced into receivership in 1931 and was subsequently taken over by the Minnesota Ontario Paper Company which in turn was purchased by Boise Cascade in 1965. A new kraft mill was constructed in 1970-71.

The international bridge, which joined Fort Frances with International Falls in 1912, was originally constructed so that the first portion could be raised to allow the passage of steamboats. When the dream of a canal system joining Lake Superior with Lake of the Woods vanished, the bridge was rebuilt.

Farming has been a major part of the economy since the early 1890's, long before the land on the Minnesota side of the Rainy River was cultivated. In 1876, 20 townships in the area were surveyed and parceled out in 160 acre lots to settlers free of charge. They were allowed to purchase an additional 80 acres of adjoining land at $1 per acre.

The town of Fort Frances was incorporated on April 11, 1903. Previously it had been a part of the Municipality of Alberton (1891-1903). This area was a part of the disputed territory claimed by both Ontario and Manitoba between 1859 and 1871. Fort Frances has been a part of the territorial distict of Rainy River since 1909, and has been the center of the Provincial Judicial District serving that area since that time.

In addition to industry and agriculture, Fort Frances is well established as a gateway to one of the finest wilderness and recreation areas of Canada.

INTERNATIONAL FALLS

The first white settler to build on the location of present day International Falls was a Scottish prospector named Alexander Baker. He arrived on the scene in 1870 after paddling all the way from Lake Superior and chose a site overlooking Koochiching Falls for the construction of his log cabin. Here he lived until his death September 14, 1899, at the age of 72. The tract of land to which he laid claim included much of the present day Mando Paper Mill site and some of the business district and residential area. Because this part of Minnesota had not been surveyed, it took ten years to clear the title to the homestead.

Courtesy Minnesota Historical Society

Alexander Baker, first settler at International Falls, and his home.

C.J. Rockwood, of Minneapolis, bought all of the Baker claim with the exception of the one acre on which the cabin was located (Baker's Acre) for $6000 in 1892. He had recognized the water power potential of the falls. Rockwood, in turn, sold out in 1900 to E.W. Backus and W.F. Brooks, who were already well established in the lumber business in Minnesota.

Joseph Baker, a nephew of the founder of the village, arrived from Scotland in 1881. He was destined to become the first postmaster, the first bandmaster, and the first Justice of the Peace of Koochiching (the original name for International Falls).

Milestones in the history of the village include:

1894 - The construction of the first school with L.A. Ogaard as the teacher.

1901 - Construction of the Canadian Northern Railroad to Fort Frances.

1902 - A fire very nearly destroyed the entire village.

1903 - Dr. M.E. Withrow established his medical practice.

1904 - R.S. McDonald arrived from Grand Rapids and cleared 240 acres of land which was soon to become part of the townsite.

1905 - A contract was let for the construction of the dam. A wagon and footbridge was completed. A telephone exchange became operational with sixty instruments.

1907 - The Minnesota and International Railroad and the Duluth Winnipeg and Pacific reached the border town.

1910, 1911 - Insulate was first produced.

1914 - The manufacture of paper was begun.

1939-40 - Plant Mix Bituminous surface applied to gravel highways leading into town - 1½ inches. [Some oil treatment in previous years]

A 1906 edition of the International Falls Echo boasted of a business community which included -

four general stores	*1 feed store*
four lawyers	*1 blacksmith shop*
two barber shops	*2 tailor shops.*

Courtesy Minnesota Historical Society

Main street, International Falls, 1902.

Although International Falls had a reputation as a "rough and lively border town", the first murder was not recorded until 1907. The killing was the result of a quarrel between two black men.

Before the coming of the railroad, travel was extremely difficult in this part of the world. We are told of one family which moved with all their worldly possessions (about a railroad carful) from New Prague, Minnesota, to Koochiching in 1894. They first traveled by railroad to Duluth. There they transferred with their goods to a freight boat and headed for Port Arthur (Thunder Bay). At Port Arthur they again unloaded and boarded the Canadian Pacific Railroad for Rat Portage (Kenora). Here, all their goods were transferred to boats in which they crossed the Lake of the Woods. They then journeyed up the Rainy River to Fort Frances. A few weeks later they crossed the river to Koochiching. The journey from New Prague to Fort Frances took fifteen days and included loading and unloading all their possessions four times!

Before the coming of the railroad in 1907, travel, whenever possible was by boat in summer and dog team in winter, however, it was often necessary or more practical to simply cut across country from such cities as Bemidji, Grand Rapids, or Big Falls (then called Ripple) - the latter served as terminal point for the M and I railroad from 1905 to 1907. The trails were often poorly marked and led across huge bogs and a dozen or more streams. Hoards of flies and mosquitoes were an added threat in summer and cold and snow were the enemies during the winter months. Although there is no authenticated record of wolves attacking or killing these early travelers, they often followed them and were at least a psychological threat!

Travelers from Duluth and the Iron Range towns of Minnesota could go by rail as far as Tower and then portage to Harding on Crane Lake, from where they could travel the remainder of the journey by water.

As we journey by air or by auto to the Lake of the Woods area today, we can scarcely imagine the hardships endured by these early travelers. Next time you drive from Blackduck to Baudette or International Falls, try to visualize *walking* across those huge bogs or through the dark cedar swamps!

KENORA

Because Kenora has been such an important center of activity for the Lake of the Woods ever since the first trading post was established at Rat Portage in 1836, we have already told much about the history and development of the community. We have seen the impact of the coming of the railroad in 1881 and the gold rush of the last decade of that century. We have traced the movement of the gigantic rafts of logs - drawn as if by a magnet to the sawmills at the north end of the Lake. We have also told of the lengthy and sometimes almost humorous struggle between the Provinces of Ontario and Manitoba for this territory. And so, having already devoted so much of this history to the story of this community, we will limit ourselves here to a discussion of the Kenora of today.

Kenora is very much a product of its environment. Not only is it located at the outlet of the Lake of the Woods, but it is literally surrounded by smaller lakes - and some not so small. The Chamber of Commerce boasts that 40,000 lakes lie within its service area. Even though Kenora has been the center of the logging and lumbering industry for this part of Canada ever since 1880, it is still rich in timber resources. And the gold discovered at the end of the last century continues to be mined. Thus the Kenora economy is based on tourism, wood products, and mining.

Illustrative of the impact of tourism on the area is the fact that more than 10,000 boats are registered in Kenora, ninety percent of which are powered by 10 h.p. motors or larger. Resorts and other tourist facilities abound and vary in size from the family operated facility to convention center size resorts and hotels. The community is also the service center for several thousands of privately owned cabins.

Logging remains a major industry and wood products are the chief output of the community's industries. The Ontario-Minnesota mill is among Canada's largest producers of paper.

The gold rush of the 1890's had a great deal to do with the growth of Rat Portage and had a lasting effect on its industrial and commercial development even though the mining operations faded in this century. Sky-rocketing gold prices in the 1970's, however, have spurred a revival of mining operations and Kenora is now the mineral center for a region stretching two hundred miles to the north and east.

Kenora is also the center of government for that district. This not only means employment for many of the residents but brings Canadians to the city on governmental business from many miles around.

It still seems a paradox that this center for industry, commerce and government with a population of more than 10,000, exists in the midst of a vast wilderness - still largely unspoiled. It never seems quite right to travel north on the Lake of the Woods across expanses of water and then through channels winding among the thousands of wooded islands - being careful not to get lost - and then suddenly come in view of the city of Kenora. Both worlds have remained remarkably compatable, with fairly large concentrations of moose, bear, deer, and all kinds of wild life within only a few minutes of the city!

MORSON

Morson is the southern gateway to Sabaskong Bay of Lake of the Woods. The village has been the outgrowth of an Indian Reserve and the Dalseg enterprises, which include a shopping centre, building supply centre, hardware store, gift shop, clothing store, bottle shop, gas station, and marina. Over the years, Dalsegs have also provided a trading center for the Indian population, particularly those who live in the Grassy Reserve. The community also includes a school. A government dock with public access and parking is located four miles north of the community on the Bay. Morson itself is connected with the Lake by the Big Grassy River.

The community is named for a native family by the name of Morrison. The founder of the family, Jonathan Morrison (part French) lived to be 109 years of age and is remembered by many from this part of the Lake. He could relate first hand many stories from the 19th century. For example, he could recall the days before the construction of the Norman Dam when he could literally step across the bay at Morson in front of the old Dalseg store location.

The Dalseg enterprises were started by Maurice Dalseg, an uncle of Norman Dalseg, the president of the company today. The first store was also a trading post and was located down river from the Dalseg Super Market and back from the shore about a half mile from the buildings used as a headquarters for the Dalseg operations prior to the construction of their new facilities in 1962.

Other pioneer families included John Quick, Sr., John Almers, Sr., S.T. Swenson, Anton Eide, Pete Odegård, Nels Olson, Knute Halverson, Nick Brusven, Norval Brusven, Oscar Brusven, Ruben DeWar, Harold Hanson, George Green, Ed Rodegard, Aron Ostlund, George Valland, Grundy Danielson, Pete DeWar, and O.C. Hanson. The latter was the father of Phil Hanson, Owner of Hanson's Resort by the Government Warf. Phil Hanson's mother was the first teacher in the Morson school.

The road to Morson came in relays. The first stretch started at Sleeman and ended at Gameland, then went on to just south of Bergland. It then continued to Minahico and out to Taylor's Bay (an outlet for tourist camps and commercial fishing). The road finally reached Hanson's Cafe corner in 1929 and came across to the Indian Reserve in 1933. It reached Elnore Bay in 1939 - across from the original Dalseg operations. The bridge across the Big Grassy River and the bridge by the Dalseg Super Market were constructed in 1945.

Although a small settlement, Morson is considerably older than Nestor Falls or Sioux Narrows, and has played a significant role in the history of Lake of the Woods.

The author's father, Richard Lund, with two Sabaskong Bay muskies taken in 1912 near the present location of the government wharf at Morson.

NESTOR FALLS

Located on Highway 71 between the border and Sioux Narrows, Nestor Falls is a tourist center and gateway for the eastern Sabaskong Bay portion of Lake of the Woods. Although a small community, it serves as a trade center for dozens of resorts and hundreds of private camps. Originally a natural falls, it has always been a favorite fishing spot. The author's father told of catching muskies or large northerns on virtually every cast here early in the 1900's. Walleyes were easy prey to frogs fished near the bottom in the holes at the foot of the falls.

Resorts and commercial development sprang up with the coming of the highway from the south in 1933. For a few years Nestor Falls was literally "the end of the road" The community also serves as a gateway to Crow Lake.

Nestor Falls has a pontoon plane base and boasts an excellent wilderness airport as well.

Nestor Falls Airport.

SIOUX NARROWS

Located 90 miles north of the border at International Falls and 35 miles south of the junction of Highway 71 with Trans Canada Highway 17, Sioux Narrows is a trade center for the resort industry and the hundreds of private cabins in the area. It boasts a winter population of 350 but a summer population of more than 5,000. Sioux Narrows has an airport with a grass runway which is usually in good condition even though unlicensed at this writing.

The village receives its name from a massacre here of a band of Sioux by the Ojibway during the 18th century. The narrows itself is spanned by the world's longest single span wooden bridge.

The author's father, Richard Lund, [far right] and friends at Nestor Falls in 1912.

The community really came into being with the opening of Highway 71 from Nestor Falls to Kenora in 1936. It is ideally located for all kinds of hunting and fishing and is the lake trout capital of Lake of the Woods.

VILLAGE OF RAINY RIVER

Located across the river from Baudette, the village of Rainy River is the gateway to Canada for those visiting southern and western Sabaskong Bay or the eastern approach to Big Traverse. It is joined to Baudette by a toll bridge which was constructed in 1960; prior to that date a ferry service was operated on the river by Frank Watson.

The Hudson's Bay Company operated a post not far from the village site near the mouth of the Rainy River most of the time from 1794 to 1893. It was originally constructed by H.B.C. employee Thomas Norn, and occupied the next year by John McKay, who described the post as being located on "one of the beautifulest rivers I ever saw in this country." Just two years later, McKay and his men were transferred to the Red River area. In 1798, the Hudson's Bay Company sent John Cobb to "the McKay House". but when he arrived he found that employees of the Northwest Trading Company had plundered the post and burned down "the men's house". Because of the severe competition from the French, the post was not again occupied until 1826. In later years (after 1832) it was referred to as "Hungry House". (see page

The village of Rainy River had its beginnings as a saw mill town and was first called "Beaver Mills". The Rainy River Lumber Company had a large operation here from the turn-of-the-century to 1911, when it was dismantled. In 1913, Shevlin-Clarke, Ltd. erected a mill. Both operations were located here because of the coming of the railroad (at the start of this century) and the Canadian National is still a major employer. Logging and lumbering also remain important to the community while agriculture, tourism, and the Arctic Cat Industry help diversify the economy. Although most tourists who enter Canada through the village of Rainy River are headed for the Lake of the Woods area, the river itself - from which the community takes its name - is a magnificent stream and a real asset. John McDonald, a clerk and trader with the Hudson's Bay Company, said of Rainy River, "This is deemed the most beautiful river in the Northwest."

Courtesy Minnesota Historical Society

Rainy River scene between Baudette and the village of Rainy River - 1905.

WARROAD

Warroad has been a White Man's town since the 1890's, but an Indian village was located on the same site - at the mouth of the Warroad River - shortly after the coming of the Ojibway to the area in the 1700's. It is likely that the predecessors to the Ojibway also headquartered here.

The name given both the river and the village could hardly be more appropriate inasmuch as they are the northern terminal of the war path between the prairies and the Lake of the Woods, over which the Ojibway and the Sioux raided each other for generations. No doubt other war parties traveled the route during earlier centuries when the predecessors to the Chippewa and the Sioux inhabited the area. The war road ran westward from the river along the gravel ridge which once formed the shore of Lake Agassiz. During times of peace and after the coming of the white man, the trail meant a convenient summer route to the west, or even to the north once the Red River was reached.

The Indian name for the site was "Ka-Beck-a-Nung", meaning - "end of the trail". The site was ideal for fur trading and we know that the American Fur Trading Company operated a post at the mouth of the river at least as early as 1822.

Henry Schoolcraft, in 1824, mentioned the site as one of many where fur trading could be carried on within the limits of the Indian Agency under his supervision.

Other trading posts followed over the years. Among the operators were Teien and Engelbritson in the 1880's and early 1890's, Duncan Begg in the 1890's and Jake Laughlin in 1896. John Ka-Ka-Geshick, the legendary Chippewa Medicine Man, recalled a Hudson's Bay Post "when he was a boy" on property owned in later years by the Robberstad family. It is believed by the people of Warroad who knew him that Ka-Ka-Gesick was born in 1842 and no later than 1844. When he died on December 8, 1968, it was accepted in the community that he was at least 124 years old! John

Ka-Ka-Gesick was a living history, and after his death, Muskeg Bay was renamed in his honor.

Warroad has continued to play an important role in the history of Lake of the Woods since the fur trading days. Even before the turn of the century, it shared in the logging and lumbering boom. It still serves as the chief gateway for Americans to the North West Angle. At this writing, regular boat service continues to bring mail and passengers from Warroad to this northern most point of "the lower forty-eight states".

Main street, Warroad; about 1912. Left to right: Hotel, Soderstrom, Prop.; Barber Shop and Pool Room; Restaurant; Rooming House; Clothing Store; Holland Drug Store; Hotel, Peter Ornes, Prop.; Groceries, John Stein, Prop.; Dr. Parker Drug Store. Dentist and doctor lived above.

Wood products remain a mainstay of the Warroad economy. The Marvin Industries deliver their lumber and other products made of wood throughout the Upper Midwest. Warroad also manufactures insulating glass and (appropriately) boasts a hockey stick factory.

Agriculture is a significant part of the Warroad economy and tourism is big business here as elsewhere around the lake.

Warroad is a relatively young community, built on the site of centuries of Indian history.

Chief John Ka-Ka-Gesick

KEEWATIN

The Indian word "Keewatin" describes the location of this village as "at the north end of the lake". Originally, along with its neighbor, Kenora, it was part of the area called Rat Portage; it was the gateway for the Indian Trappers to muskrat country. Not only did the Indians pass through here on their way north, but the muskrats themselves portaged back and forth between the Lake of the Woods and the Winnipeg River.

You will recall that it was John Mather - the pioneer in finance and logging - who in 1879 named the village "Keewatin Mills" and limited the Rat Portage designation to present day Kenora. Keewatin was John Mather's base of operations.

It was also in 1879 that Mather and four associates incorporated the Keewatin Lumbering and Manufacturing Company Limited. Construction of a saw mill (to be operated by water power) began the same year. The planing mill - also operated by water power - was built in 1879 and 1880. John Mather's sons, "D.L." and "R.A..", actually operated the mills. The sawmill burned down in 1905, but the planing mill continued for several years.

A tie mill was constructed in 1903 for the purpose of providing the railroad with sawed ties instead of "hewn" ties. The tie mill was transferred to the Backus Brooks Company in 1906 and later to the Keewatin Lumber Company. Since 1968, Boise Cascade has operated a tie and stud mill on the same site.

The Dick and Banning Company built a lumber mill in Keewatin which was in operation from about 1882 to 1893. In 1899, the Ottawa Gold Milling and Mining Company took over the site and constructed a large reduction works and stamp mill. The ore was transported by railroad from the company's "Sakoose" mine to Keewatin via Dyment. The operation was short lived; it closed in 1900.

The Mather family was also instrumental in the construction of flour mills in Keewatin. John Mather was Vice President of the Lake of the Woods Milling Company, which was organized in 1887 and began its operations in Keewatin the next year. By 1903, when it was sold to Greenshields and Russell, the company was among the largest in Canada.

Mather then organized a rival company, the Keewatin Flour Mill Company, Ltd., but it was bought out by the Lake of the Woods Milling Company in 1906, just before it went into operation. The Company sold its product under the "Five Roses" label. In 1967, Keewatin suffered its greatest tragedy with the destruction of the mill by fire. One hundred and fifty persons were suddenly unemployed. The mill site was given to the city.

It might at first seem surprising that Keewatin would be a milling center, but it was the nearest source of power to the Manitoba wheat fields before the turn of the century.

Today, Keewatin must depend on its environment for survival; logging, lumbering, and tourism.

Since 1972, an electrically driven boat lift has made it possible to transport boats up to 30 feet in length between Lake of the Woods and the Winnipeg River in eight minutes.

Perhaps the community's greatest asset is its beautiful location on a 200 acre peninsula bounded on all sides but the West by two bays of the Lake of the Woods and a large bay of the Winnipeg River. The city is built on a ridge between the river and the lake and it is this ridge which has made possible the water power which brought industry to the community. Twenty-one feet separate the water levels of the lake and the river.

In spite of the industrial misfortunes which had befallen Keewatin, geography has assured Keewatin's future.

CHAPTER XIII
Suggestions For Fishing
Lake Of The Woods

Because of the abundance of fish in the Lake, there is little excuse for returning to the dock without a full stringer during most of the spring and summer season. Yet, just putting in the time is not enough. Your favorite lures and techniques will probably work here as well as in any lake, but *where* you fish is critically important. Fish will change their location and feeding habits with the season and success with a given technique in one location in May does not guarantee fish in the same place in July. Lake of the Woods differs from most lakes in that rising early to be out on the lake at dawn may not be worth the effort. Mid morning, noon, and evening are most productive. Because of the great variety of depths and types of bottom, structure is very important. Perhaps the most valuable tool in which you can invest is the electronic depth finder. It doesn't really matter very much whether or not you ever learn to "see fish" on the indicator, but it is important that you keep your boat at the depth where they are biting. There are few lakes where the bottom is more irregular or where the shoreline tells you less about the depth. Weather seems to be a more important factor here than on most lakes. When a cold front moves in, fishing usually drops off severly for at least 24 hours.

WALLEYE PIKE (pickerel)

Lake of the Woods ranks among the top ten walleye lakes of North America on any man's list. Live bait is the most productive, but your favorite artificial lure will produce. Baited jigs (with minnow, leech, or a piece of nightcrawler) are particularly effective. The new rigs which combine a small hook with a sliding sinker or split shot and are trolled at very slow speeds with a night crawler, leech, or minnow as bait are also very effective. The "old stand by" is the Lake of the Woods spinner with a minnow hooked for trolling, usually heavily weighted to get down on the bottom.

Bottom structure is critical to walleye fishing, particularly in the summer months. Drop offs along shorelines or working around small islands or reefs is usually productive. Points of land also are usually good indicators of walleye structure. This means you will be fishing a rocky bottom much of the time and can plan on losing a great deal of tackle. Sandy shorelines and edges of weed beds are productive on summer evenings. Work the shorelines where the wind has been blowing in during the day. It is important to note the depth at which the walleyes are feeding and then maintain that depth when trolling or drifting. This is especially important when working around reefs or along irregular shorelines. Walleyes are school fish; when you get one, try that area for sometime. However, if a spot is not productive, move. It may be worthwhile coming back later but it is often a waste of time waiting for them to come in.

In the spring, reefs are seldom productive. The fish are more scattered and are usually found in bays or along sandy shorelines or in areas near where they have spawned. Mouths of rivers or inlets are also productive. In early spring, seek waters which have been warmed by the sun. Use small baits.

Trophy small mouths.

This live box gives testimony not only to good fishing but also to the variety of fish available in the Lake of the Woods.

Fall fishing for walleyes is not very good in the island portions of the lake. Concentrate on rivers, inlets, and Big Traverse.

Fishing through the ice can be very productive, especially in early winter and during March and early April (just before the Canadian season closes). Walleyes are usually found in between eight and twelve feet of water on flats or sandy bottoms. They will also bite at night in shallower water along sandy shores.

Many studies have been made of the stomach contents of walleyes. On Lake of the Woods as high as 90% of their diet is perch. (late summer and fall) Shiner minnows make up 10% of the diet at the most (early summer).[1]

Walleyes feed on or close to the bottom; therefore, it is important that whatever bait you use is presented at that depth. This means very slow trolling or drifting. It is often helpful to troll backwards; this not only slows down the boat but keeps lines out of the motor. Bouncing the bait along the bottom may cost you a lot of tackle, but it will also fill your stringer.

NORTHERN PIKE

Although not as popular for eating as the walleye, the northern is far more fun to catch. Actually, there is nothing wrong with the flavor of the fish; it is just that the bones are a nuisance. The bones are not a problem if the fish are baked, ground into patties, or pickled. If care is taken, filets for frying can be de-boned quite satisfactorily by cutting out the strip of flesh containing the "Y" bones.

The northern pike is "a big eater" and usually strikes and fights as though he were starved. Northerns are often caught while fishing for walleyes. If you start catching them while trolling, speed up the motor and you will probably catch more. Bigger northerns are often caught while trolling very fast. If you have not used this technique before, try trolling at least twice as fast as you troll for walleyes.

For both northerns and muskies, try trolling one bait in the wake of the boat and the others farther back.

Casting is not only a productive method, but it is more fun. Choosing spots that look like they may shelter a northern makes the sport seem almost like hunting. Rushes, weed beds, and rocky shorelines are good places to try. Usually the shore where the wind has been blowing in is the best bet. The bigger the waves the better. If casting doesn't work, try trolling. If that doesn't work, try deeper water. You may find northerns as deep as twenty-five feet, even early in the season. Spring fishing is usually better in or near the mouths of streams or inlets where the fish have spawned or where late spawning bait fish or suckers may still be active. Northerns will take most any walleye bait, but spoons, buck tails, large spinners, and plugs are often better for casting or fast trolling. Live bait is consistently good, but requires more patience. If you use a bobber, make certain it is just large enough to hold up the bait so that the fish will not feel it when he strikes. Unless the northern hooks himself when he takes the bait, you will have to wait for him to swallow it. The rule of thumb here is to wait until after his initial rush and set the hook when he takes off on his second run. Monofilament is less visible than a wire leader but will soon be sawed off by the northern's sharp teeth unless it is at least 20# test.

Northerns are less affected by weather than walleyes. They are not a school fish, but when you find one, others are probably along the same area. If you don't have action, move. Changing baits will probably make less difference than changing locations and style of fishing.

Ice fishing for northerns can be very productive early and late in the winter season. Use large minnows for bait.

[1] [Smith & Muth] The burbot Fishery in Lake of the Woods, U of M, 1974

Trophy small mouths caught by Stan Edin in a small lake on the Alneau Peninsula.

Greg Hayenga with a "baking-size" northern.

SMALL MOUTH BASS

Don't judge the eating quality of the small mouth by its cousin the large mouth bass. They may be "look alikes" but their habitats are exact opposites. Whereas the large mouth can thrive over muddy bottoms and in heavy weed beds, the small mouth demands clear water and prefers rocky shorelines or structure. There is a world of difference in the eating. Pound for pound they are probably the best fighters in the Lake of the Woods. They are also the most difficult to find.

Up until mid June they will be found on or near their spawning grounds. Look for sandy bottoms near rock structure and fairly shallow water. Also, any time of the year, watch the shoreline for small rocks - about egg size. These rocky bottoms provide the crawfish and hatching insects on which the small mouths feed. Although they are often caught while fishing walleyes, casting is usually the best technique. Jigs, small plugs, spoons, and spinners are the most productive. Live bait fished on the bottom is also good. Bass like leeches, night crawlers, and minnows - in that order.

Small mouths are deceptive fighters and if you don't keep a tight line when they go into their aerial acrobatics you will only have the thrill left.

MUSKELLUNGE

The muskie is perhaps the most exciting and legendary fish in the Lake. Although walleye, northern, and small mouth fishing have remained good down through the years, the muskellunge population has suffered. They simply do not reproduce as well and are therefore more vulnerable to heavy fishing. Lake of the Woods has become world famous as muskie waters and many record fish have been taken.

Bruce Lund with Sabaskong Bay Muskie.

Muskies are more hunted than fished. It is a sport all in its own. More muskies are probably caught "by accident" while fishing other varieties, but there are techniques which increase the odds considerably. First, it is important to learn to recognize the areas where they are likely to be found. Contrary to popular opinion, they do not spend most of their time in shallow water. However, since shallow water cover is easier to recognize, most fishing consists of casting along shorelines or around the mouths of streams and inlets. Trolling (fast) along weed beds in deeper water is really more productive.

Big fish are often caught on small baits, but most muskie fishermen use magnum size spinners, spoons and plugs. Record books would indicate that most large muskies are taken on bucktail spinners. This is probably because these baits are more often trolled than cast. But casting is fun and many fishermen would rather catch half as many fish and have the thrill of seeing the water explode or the shadow of a monster follow the bait and then disappear under the boat. It's no sport for a weak heart! If you prefer to cast, try very fast or at least eratic retrieves.

There is no doubt that several record breaking muskies are still swimming in Lake of the Woods waters.

CRAPPIES

There are many better crappie lakes, but there is something very special about the big, black slabs that come from Lake of the Woods. In the spring they can be found in large schools in shallow water along rocky points, on the deep side of big shore rocks, on the edge of floating bogs, or around trees which may have fallen into the water. After spawning, they move into deeper water and can be fished along weed beds, especially in the evening. They seem to move into even deeper water in the fall and winter - about 25 to 40 feet.

Ontario had no limit on crappies until recent years. In the 1960's some excellent winter crappie fishing was discovered and they were soon being caught by the pickup truck load - literally. Crappie fishing hasn't been the same in those parts of the Lake since. Unlike their southern cousins they are slow growing and do not reproduce as rapidly in these northern waters. It takes eight to ten years to grow a "slab size" crappie.

Small minnows are the most common bait, but small jigs are also good. For winter fishing, it is better to bait the jig with a wax worm, "mousie" worm, or very small minnow. Crappies are usually delicate feeders and the slightest touch of your bait or movement of the bobber signals the time to strike.

LAKE TROUT

This fish of the far north is pretty much limited in Lake of the Woods to Whitefish Bay. Although many lakes in this part of Ontario are more productive, few if any produce so many large lake trout.

Because the trout demand cold water, they can be fished near the surface only in the spring and late fall (or through the ice in winter). Summer fishing is limited to techniques which present the bait at seventy feet or lower. From the time the ice goes out through the first week of June, lake trout may be taken by trolling in relatively shallow water (fifteen to thirty five feet deep) with most any lure that has a chrome finish or resembles a small tulibee. Jigs baited with minnows are also productive. Trout are often fished from shore this time of the year with pieces of sucker meat or dead smelt sewed on the hook. If you use sucker meat, be sure to scale it first. If you can't get suckers, try large sucker minnows and squash them. When fishing from shore, you may have to take the bait out to the end of your line by boat and then let it settle to the bottom. Lake trout often feed like scavengers.

The lake trout is a magnificent fish, however, it tastes best when fried fresh. It seems to lose flavor rapidly through freezing (even when frozen in ice). Try smoking the next trout you bring home.

Jerry Hayenga shows off trophy Lake Trout from the cold waters of Whitefish Bay.

CHAPTER XIV
Some Final Facts
About Our Lake

●The Lake includes

-1,980 square miles, 2/3 of which lies in Ontario and Manitoba. Of this, 1,485 square miles is water.

-a complete watershed area of 27,000 square miles.

-65,000 miles of shoreline (more than Lake Superior).

-14,000 islands (more than any other lake on the North American Continent).

-an average depth of 26 feet, including Big Traverse Bay with an average depth of about 30' and extensive deep areas in Clearwater and Whitefish Bays with depths of more than 150 feet. A depth of 216 feet has been recorded northwest of the Three Sisters Islands in Whitefish Bay.

-At its widest, a 65 mile width from north to south and a 55 mile width from east to west.

●Rainy River is the principal tributary of the Lake of the Woods and furnishes about ¾ of the lake's water.

●The outlet of the Lake is the Winnipeg River into which water flows through three "shoots". This river flows north into Lake Winnipeg, Nelson River, and Hudson Bay of the Arctic Ocean.

●Three dams near Kenora and the dam on the Rainy River at International Falls and Fort Frances control the lake level. Although the water level is regulated by "the International Lake of the Woods Control Board", extremes have not always been avoided; flooding occurred in 1950 and low levels caused problems in 1973. The upper and lower levels of storage are intended to be 1061.25 feet above sea level and 1056 feet a.s.l. It is not uncommon for the lake level to vary as much as three or four feet in any year. Water levels may change by two or more feet with a radical change in the wind. The thousands of islands act like little dams which keep the new water level from shifting back very rapidly and result in currents in the narrows between islands long after a wind has gone down or changed direction.

●The wild rice crop fluctuates a great deal from year to year, partly because of changing water levels. The crop usually covers from six to eight thousand acres.

●The Lake of the Woods lies within the Canadian Shield. It is thought to have been created during four ice ages. Soil layers are relatively thin with major outcroppings of bedrock. One of the marvels of the Lake is how the giant pines seem to take root in bare rock with very little soil for nourishment or support.

●Each of the four segments of the Lake of the Woods is different from the others in shoreline, bottom, depth, etc. While waters are deep and clear in Whitefish Bay, they are often clouded with silt and colored brown by swamp and bog water in southern parts of the Lake.

●It is estimated that the dams at Kenora raised the lake level three to six feet. Before the lake level was raised, it was possible to go by horse and buggy from Warroad to the Rainy River on one long, sandy beach.

Gordon Dezell and Neil Krough with a box full of winter walleyes and a northern.

Wiener roast at sunset.

Jack Carlson weighs in a 30 lb. muskie.

BIBLIOGRAPHY

Brycem, George, Lake of the Woods; It's History, Geology, Mining, and Manufacturing, 1897.

Burpee, L.J., The Lake of the Woods Tragedy, 1903.

Centennial Review, Kenora, 1936.

Cooper, John Montgomery, Notes on the Ethnology of the Otchipwe of Lake of the Woods and Rainy Lake, 1936.

Eschambault, Antoine d', Discover of Lake of the Woods, 1932.

Gale, Edward Chenery, From Kenora to Fort Frances with Edward C. Gale, 1943.

Hinckley, Ira W., Rainy Lake Legends, 1953.

Hinckley, Ira W., Way Back When, 1949.

International Joint Commission [U.S. and Canada], Final Report of the International Joint Commission on the Lake of the Woods Reference, 1917.

Margy, Pierre, Pierre Gautier de La Verendrye de'couvry a' l'quest du Lac Superior et occupe par des posts, 1886.

Minnesota Interim Commission of the Lake of the Woods and Rainy Lake Area - 1969 [to the Minnesota State Legislature]

Muth, Kenneth and Smith, Lloyd, The Burbot Fishing in Lake of the Woods, U of M, 1974.

North American Boundary Commission [Between the United States and the Possessions of Great Britain from the Lake of the Woods to the Summit of the Rocky Mountains, 1872.

Nute, Grace, Rainy Lake Country, 1943.

Schaefer, Francis James, Fort St. Charles: The Massacre in the Lake of the Woods and the Discoveries Connected Therewith, 1909.

U.S. Congress House Committee on the Judiciary, Lake of the Woods, 1954.

U.S. Engineer Department, International Boundary Waters, 1930.

Warren, William W., History of the Ojibways, Minnesota Historical Collection, Volume 5.

TREATY No. 3

BETWEEN

HER MAJESTY THE QUEEN

AND THE

SAULTEAUX TRIBE

OF THE

OJIBBEWAY INDIANS

AT THE

NORTHWEST ANGLE ON THE LAKE OF THE WOODS
WITH ADHESIONS

ORDER IN COUNCIL SETTING UP
COMMISSION FOR TREATY 3

The Committee have had under consideration the memorandum dated 19th April, 1871, from the Hon. the Secretary of State for the provinces submitting with reference to his report of the 17th of the same month that the Indians mentioned in the last paragraph of that report and with whom it will be necessary first to deal occupy the country from the water shed of Lake Superior to the north west angle of the Lake of the Woods and from the American border to the height of land from which the streams flow towards Hudson's Bay.

That they are composed of Saulteaux and Lac Seul Indians of the Ojibbeway Nation, and number about twenty-five hundred men, women and children, and, retaining what they desire in reserves at certain localities where they fish for sturgeon, would, it is thought be willing to surrender for a certain annual payment their lands to the Crown. That the American Indians to the south of them surrendered their lands to the Government of the United States for an annual payment which has been stated to him (but not on authority) to amount to ten dollars per head for each man, woman and child of which six dollars is paid in goods and four in money. That to treat with these Indians with advantage he recommends that Mr. Simon J. Dawson of the Department of Public Works and Mr. Robert Pither of the Hudson's Bay Company's service be associated with Mr. Wemyss M. Simpson—and further that the presents which were promised the Indians last year and a similar quantity for the present year should be collected at Fort Francis not later than the middle of June also that four additional suits of Chiefs' clothes and flags should be added to those now in store at Fort Francis— and further that a small house and store for provisions should be constructed at Rainy River at the site and of the dimensions which Mr. Simpson may deem best—that the assistance of the Department of Public Works will be necessary should his report be adopted in carrying into effect the recommendations therein made as to provisions, clothes and construction of buildings.

He likewise submits that it will be necessary that the sum of Six Thousand dollars in silver should be at Fort Francis subject to the Order of the above named Commissioners on the fifteenth day of June next—And further recommends that in the instructions to be given to them they should be directed to make the best arrangements in their power but authorized if need be to give as much as twelve dollars a family for each family not exceeding five—with such small Sum in addition where the family exceeds five as the Commissioners may find necessary —Such Subsidy to be made partly in goods and provisions and partly in money or wholly in goods and provisions should the Commissioners so decide for the surrender of the lands described in the earlier part of this report.

The Committee concur in the foregoing recommendations and submit the same for Your Excellency's approval.

Signed: Charles Tupper

25 April/71
Approved:
    L

TREATY No. 3

ARTICLES OF A TREATY made and concluded this third day of October, in the year of Our Lord one thousand eight hundred and seventy-three, between Her Most Gracious Majesty the Queen of Great Britain and Ireland, by Her Commissioners, the Honourable Alexander Morris, Lieutenant-Governor of the Province of Manitoba and the North-west Territories; Joseph Alfred Norbert Provencher and Simon James Dawson, of the one part, and the Saulteaux Tribe of the Ojibway Indians, inhabitants of the country within the limits hereinafter defined and described, by their Chiefs chosen and named as hereinafter mentioned, of the other part.

Whereas the Indians inhabiting the said country have, pursuant to an appointment made by the said Commissioners, been convened at a meeting at the north-west angle of the Lake of the Woods to deliberate upon certain matters of interest to Her Most Gracious Majesty, of the one part, and the said Indians of the other.

And whereas the said Indians have been notified and informed by Her Majesty's said Commissioners that it is the desire of Her Majesty to open up for settlement, immigration and such other purpose as to Her Majesty may seem meet, a tract of country bounded and described as hereinafter mentioned, and to obtain the consent thereto of Her Indian subjects inhabiting the said tract, and to make a treaty and arrange with them so that there may be peace and good will between them and Her Majesty and that they may know and be assured of what allowance they are to count upon and receive from Her Majesty's bounty and benevolence.

And whereas the Indians of the said tract, duly convened in council as aforesaid, and being requested by Her Majesty's said Commissioners to name certain Chiefs and Headmen, who should be authorized on their behalf to conduct such negotiations and sign any treaty to be founded thereon, and to become responsible to Her Majesty for their faithful performance by their respective bands of such obligations as shall be assumed by them, the said Indians have thereupon named the following persons for that purpose, that is to say:—

KEK-TA-PAY-PI-NAIS (Rainy River.)
KITCHI-GAY-KAKE (Rainy River.)
NOTE-NA-QUA-HUNG (North-West Angle.)
NAWE-DO-PE-NESS (Rainy River.)
POW-WA-SANG (North-West Angle.)
CANDA-COM-IGO-WE-NINIE (North-West Angle.)
PAPA-SKO-GIN (Rainy River.)
MAY-NO-WAH-TAW-WAYS-KIONG (North-West Angle.)
KITCHI-NE-KA-LE-HAN (Rainy River.)
SAH-KATCH-EWAY (Lake Seul.)
MUPA-DAY-WAH-SIN (Kettle Falls.)
ME-PIE-SIES (Rainy Lake, Fort Frances.)
OOS-CON-NA-GEITH (Rainy Lake.)
WAH-SHIS-KOUCE (Eagle Lake.)
KAH-KEE-Y-ASH (Flower Lake.)
GO-BAY (Rainy Lake.)
KA-MO-TI-ASH (White Fish Lake.)
NEE-SHO-TAL (Rainy River.)
KEE-JE-GO-KAY (Rainy River.)

SHĄ-SHA-GANCE (Shoal Lake.)
SHAH-WIN-ṄA-BI-NAIS (Shoal Lake.)
AY-ASH-A-WATH (Buffalo Point.)
PAY-AH-BEE-WASH (White Fish Bay.)
KAH-TAY-TAY-PA-E-CUTCH (Lake of the Woods.)

And thereupon, in open council, the different bands having presented their Chiefs to the said Commissioners as the Chiefs and Headmen for the purposes aforesaid of the respective bands of Indians inhabiting the said district hereinafter described:

And whereas the said Commissioners then and there received and acknowledged the persons so presented as Chiefs and Headmen for the purpose aforesaid of the respective bands of Indians inhabiting the said district hereinafter described;

And whereas the said Commissioners have proceeded to negotiate a treaty with the said Indians, and the same has been finally agreed upon and concluded, as follows, that is to say:—

The Saulteaux Tribe of the Ojibbeway Indians and all other the Indians inhabiting the district hereinafter described and defined, do hereby cede, release, surrender and yield up to the Government of the Dominion of Canada for Her Majesty the Queen and Her successors forever, all their rights, titles and privileges whatsoever, to the lands included within the following limits, that is to say:—

Commencing at a point on the Pigeon River route where the international boundary line between the Territories of Great Britain and the United States intersects the height of land separating the waters running to Lake Superior from those flowing to Lake Winnipeg; thence northerly, westerly and easterly along the height of land aforesaid, following its sinuosities, whatever their course may be, to the point at which the said height of land meets the summit of the watershed from which the streams flow to Lake Nepigon; thence northerly and westerly, or whatever may be its course, along the ridge separating the waters of the Nepigon and the Winnipeg to the height of land dividing the waters of the Albany and the Winnipeg; thence westerly and north-westerly along the height of land dividing the waters flowing to Hudson's Bay by the Albany or other rivers from those running to English River and the Winnipeg to a point on the said height of land bearing north forty-five degrees east from Fort Alexander, at the mouth of the Winnipeg; thence south forty-five degrees west to Fort Alexander, at the mouth of the Winnipeg; thence southerly along the eastern bank of the Winnipeg to the mouth of White Mouth River; thence southerly by the line described as in that part forming the eastern boundary of the tract surrendered by the Chippewa and Swampy Cree tribes of Indians to Her Majesty on the third of August, one thousand eight hundred and seventy-one, namely, by White Mouth River to White Mouth Lake, and thence on a line having the general bearing of White Mouth River to the forty-ninth parallel of north latitude; thence by the forty-ninth parallel of north latitude to the Lake of the Woods, and from thence by the international boundary line to the place beginning.

The tract comprised within the lines above described, embracing an area of fifty-five thousand square miles, be the same more or less. To have and to hold the same to Her Majesty the Queen, and Her successors forever.

And Her Majesty the Queen hereby agrees and undertakes to lay aside reserves for farming lands, due respect being had to lands at present cultivated by the said Indians, and also to lay aside and reserve for the benefit of the said Indians, to be administered and dealt with for them by Her Majesty's Government of the Dominion of Canada, in such a manner as shall seem best, other reserves of land in the said territory hereby ceded, which said reserves shall be

selected and set aside where it shall be deemed most convenient and advanta-
geous for each band or bands of Indians, by the officers of the said Government
appointed for that purpose, and such selection shall be so made after conference
with the Indians; provided, however, that such reserves, whether for farming
or other purposes, shall in no wise exceed in all one square mile for each family
of five, or in that proportion for larger or smaller families; and such selections
shall be made if possible during the course of next summer, or as soon thereafter
as may be found practicable, it being understood, however, that if at the time
of any such selection of any reserve, as aforesaid, there are any settlers within
the bounds of the lands reserved by any band, Her Majesty reserves the right
to deal with such settlers as She shall deem just so as not to diminish the extent
of land allotted to Indians, and provided also that the aforesaid reserves of lands,
or any interest or right therein or appurtenant thereto, may be sold, leased or
otherwise disposed of by the said Government for the use and benefit of the said
Indians, with the consent of the Indians entitled thereto first had and obtained.

And with a view to show the satisfaction of Her Majesty with the behaviour
and good conduct of Her Indians She hereby, through Her Commissioners, makes
them a present of twelve dollars for each man, woman and child belonging to
the bands here represented, in extinguishment of all claims heretofore preferred.

And further, Her Majesty agrees to maintain schools for instruction in such
reserves hereby made as to Her Government of Her Dominion of Canada may
seem advisable whenever the Indians of the reserve shall desire it.

Her Majesty further agrees with Her said Indians that within the boundary
of Indian reserves, until otherwise determined by Her Government of the
Dominion of Canada, no intoxicating liquor shall be allowed to be introduced
or sold, and all laws now in force or hereafter to be enacted to preserve Her
Indian subjects inhabiting the reserves or living elsewhere within Her North-west
Territories, from the evil influences of the use of intoxicating liquors, shall be
strictly enforced.

Her Majesty further agrees with Her said Indians that they, the said
Indians, shall have right to pursue their avocations of hunting and fishing throughout the tract surrendered as hereinbefore described, subject to such regulations as
may from time to time be made by Her Government of Her Dominion of Canada,
and saving and excepting such tracts as may, from time to time, be required or
taken up for settlement, mining, lumbering or other purposes by Her said
Government of the Dominion of Canada, or by any of the subjects thereof duly
authorized therefor by the said Government.

It is further agreed between Her Majesty and Her said Indians that such
sections of the reserves above indicated as may at any time be required for
Public Works or buildings of what nature soever may be appropriated for that
purpose by Her Majesty's Government of the Dominion of Canada, due compensation being made for the value of any improvements thereon.

And further, that Her Majesty's Commissioners shall, as soon as possible
after the execution of this treaty, cause to be taken an accurate census of all
the Indians inhabiting the tract above described, distributing them in families,
and shall in every year ensuing the date hereof, at some period in each year to
be duly notified to the Indians, and at a place or places to be appointed for that
purpose within the territory ceded, pay to each Indian person the sum of five
dollars per head yearly.

It is further agreed between Her Majesty and the said Indians that the sum
of fifteen hundred dollars per annum shall be yearly and every year expended by
Her Majesty in the purchase of ammunition and twine for nets for the use of
the said Indians.

It is further agreed between Her Majesty and the said Indians that the following articles shall be supplied to any band of the said Indians who are now

actually cultivating the soil or who shall hereafter commence to cultivate the land, that is to say: two hoes for every family actually cultivating, also one spade per family as aforesaid, one plough for every ten families as aforesaid, five harrows for every twenty families as aforesaid, one scythe for every family as aforesaid, and also one axe and one cross-cut saw, one hand-saw, one pit-saw, the necessary files, one grind-stone, one auger for each band, and also for each Chief for the use of his band one chest of ordinary carpenter's tools; also for each band enough of wheat, barley, potatoes and oats to plant the land actually broken up for cultivation by such band; also for each band one yoke of oxen, one bull and four cows; all the aforesaid articles to be given once for all for the encouragement of the practice of agriculture among the Indians.

It is further agreed between Her Majesty and the said Indians that each Chief duly recognized as such shall receive an annual salary of twenty-five dollars per annum, and each subordinate officer, not exceeding three for each band, shall receive fifteen dollars per annum; and each such Chief and subordinate officer as aforesaid shall also receive once in every three years a suitable suit of clothing; and each Chief shall receive, in recognition of the closing of the treaty, a suitable flag and medal.

And the undersigned Chiefs, on their own behalf and on behalf of all other Indians inhabiting the tract within ceded, do hereby solemnly promise and engage to strictly observe this treaty, and also to conduct and behave themselves as good and loyal subjects of Her Majesty the Queen. They promise and engage that they will in all respects obey and abide by the law, that they will maintain peace and good order between each other, and also between themselves and other tribes of Indians, and between themselves and others of Her Majesty's subjects, whether Indians or whites, now inhabiting or hereafter to inhabit any part of the said ceded tract, and that they will not molest the person or property of any inhabitants of such ceded tract, or the property of Her Majesty the Queen, or interfere with or trouble any person passing or travelling through the said tract, or any part thereof; and that they will aid and assist the officers of Her Majesty in bringing to justice and punishment any Indian offending against the stipulations of this treaty, or infringing the laws in force in the country so ceded.

IN WITNESS WHEREOF, Her Majesty's said Commissioners and the said Indian Chiefs have hereunto subscribed and set their hands at the North-West Angle of the Lake of the Woods this day and year herein first above named.

Signed by the Chiefs within named, in presence of the following witnesses, the same having been first read and explained by the Honorable James McKay:

ALEX. MORRIS, *L.G.*,
J. A. N. PROVENCHER, *Ind. Comr.*,
S. J. DAWSON,

JAMES MCKAY,
MOLYNEUX ST. JOHN,
ROBERT PITHER,
CHRISTINE V. K. MORRIS,
CHARLES NOLIN,
A. MCDONALD, *Capt.*,
  Comg. Escort to Lieut. Governor.
JAS. F. GRAHAM,
JOSEPH NOLIN,
A. MCLEOD,
GEORGE MCPHERSON, Sr.,
SEDLEY BLANCHARD,
W. FRED. BUCHANAN,
FRANK G. BECHER,

his
KEE-TA-KAY-PI-NAIS, x
mark.
his
KITCHI-GAY-KAKE, x
mark.
his
NO-TE-NA-QUA-HUNG, x
mark.
his
MAWE-DO-PE-NAIS, x
mark.
his
POW-WA-SANG, x
mark.

Alfred Codd, M.D.,
G. S. Corbault,
Pierre LeVieller,
Nicholas Chatelaine.

Canda-com-igo-wi-nine, his x mark.

May-no-wah-taw-ways-kung, his x mark.

Kitchi-ne-ka-be-han, his x mark.

Sah-katch-eway, his x mark.

Muka-day-wah-sin, his x mark.

Me-kie-sies, his x mark.

Oos-con-na-geish, his x mark.

Wah-shis-kouce, his x mark.

Kah-kee-y-ash, his x mark.

Go-bay, his x mark.

Ka-me-ti-ash, his x mark.

Nee-sho-tal, his x mark

Kee-jee-go-kay, his x mark

Sha-sha-gauce, his x mark.

Shaw-win-na-bi-nais, his x mark.

Ay-ash-a-wash, his x mark.

Pay-ah-bee-wash, his x mark.

Kah-tay-tay-pa-o-cutch, his x mark.

We, having had communication of the treaty, a certified copy whereof is hereto annexed, but not having been present at the councils held at the North West Angle of the Lake of the Woods, between Her Majesty's Commissioners, and the several Indian Chiefs and others therein named, at which the articles of the said treaty were agreed upon, hereby for ourselves and the several bands of Indians which we represent, in consideration of the provisions of the said treaty being extended to us and the said bands which we represent, transfer, surrender and relinquish to Her Majesty the Queen, Her heirs and successors, to and for the use of Her Government of Her Dominion of Canada, all our right, title and privilege whatsoever, which we, the said Chiefs and the said bands which we represent have, hold or enjoy, of, in and to the territory described and fully set out in the said articles of treaty, and every part thereof. To have and to hold the same unto and to the use of Her said Majesty the Queen, Her heirs and successors forever.

And we hereby agree to accept the several provisions, payments and reserves of the said treaty, as therein stated, and solemnly promise and engage to abide by, carry out and fulfil all the stipulations, obligations and conditions therein contained, on the part of the said Chiefs and Indians therein named, to be observed and performed; and in all things to conform to the articles of the said treaty as if we ourselves and the bands which we represent had been originally contracting parties thereto, and had been present and attached our signatures to the said treaty.

IN WITNESS WHEREOF, Her Majesty's said Commissioners and the said Indian Chiefs have hereunto subscribed and set their hands, this thirteenth day of October, in the year of Our Lord one thousand eight hundred and seventy-three.

Signed by S. J. Dawson, Esquire, one of Her Majesty's said Commissioners, for and on behalf and with the authority and consent of the Honorable Alexander Morris, Lieutenant Governor of Manitoba and the North-West Territories, and J. A. N. Provencher, Esq., the remaining two Commissioners, and himself and by the Chiefs within named, on behalf of themselves and the several bands which they represent, the same and the annexed certified copy of articles of treaty having been first read and explained in presence of the following witnesses:

    THOS. A. P. TOWERS,
    JOHN AITKEN,
    A. J. McDONALD.
    UNZZAKI.
          his
    JAS. LOGANOSH, x
          mark.
    PINLLSISE.

For and on behalf of the Commissioners, the Honorable Alexander Morris, Lieut. Governor of Manitoba and the North-West Territories, Joseph Albert Norbert Provencher, Esquire, and the undersigned

    S. J. DAWSON,
       Commissioner.
       his
    PAY-BA-MA-CHAS, x
       mark.
       his
    RE-BA-QUIN, x
       mark.
          his
    ME-TAS-SO-QUE-NE-SKANK, x
          mark.

To S. J. Dawson, Esquire, Indian Commissioner, &c., &c., &c.

Sir,—We hereby authorize you to treat with the various bands belonging to the Salteaux Tribe of the Ojibbeway Indians inhabiting the North-West Territories of the Dominion of Canada not included in the foregoing certified copy of articles of treaty, upon the same conditions and stipulations as are therein agreed upon, and to sign and execute for us and in our name and on our behalf the foregoing agreement annexed to the foregoing treaty.

North-West Angle, Lake of the Woods,   ALEX. MORRIS,
    October 4th, A.D. 1873.   *Lieutenant-Governor.*

J. A. N. PROVENCHER,
Indian Commissioner.

ADHESION BY HALFBREEDS OF RAINY RIVER AND LAKE

(A.)

This Memorandum of Agreement made and entered into this twelfth day of September one thousand eight hundred and seventy-five, between Nicholas Chatelaine, Indian interpreter at Fort Francis and the Rainy River and acting herein solely in the latter capacity for and as representing the said Half-breeds, on the one part, and John Stoughton Dennis, Surveyor General of Dominion Lands, as representing Her Majesty the Queen through the Government of the Dominion, of the other part, Witnesseth as follows:—

Whereas the Half-breeds above described, by virtue of their Indian blood, claim a certain interest or title in the lands or territories in the vicinity of Rainy Lake and the Rainy River, for the commutation or surrender of which claims they ask compensation from the Government.

And whereas, having fully and deliberately discussed and considered the matter, the said Half-breeds have elected to join in the treaty made between the Indians and Her Majesty, at the North-West Angle of the Lake of the Woods, on the third day of October, 1873, and have expressed a desire thereto, and to become subject to the terms and conditions thereof in all respects saving as hereinafter set forth.

It is now hereby agreed upon by and between the said parties hereto (this agreement, however, to be subject in all respects to approval and confirmation by the Government, without which the same shall be considered as void and of no effect), as follows, that is to say: The Half-breeds, through Nicholas Chatelaine, their Chief above named, as representing them herein, agree as follows, that is to say:—

That they hereby fully and voluntarily surrender to Her Majesty the Queen to be held by Her Majesty and Her successors for ever, any and all claim, right, title or interest which they, by virtue of their Indian blood, have or possess in the lands or territories above described, and solemnly promise to observe all the terms and conditions of the said treaty (a copy whereof, duly certified by the Honourable the Secretary of State of the Dominion has been this day placed in the hands of the said Nicholas Chatelaine).

In consideration of which Her Majesty agrees as follows, that is to say:—

That the said Half-breeds, keeping and observing on their part the terms and conditions of the said treaty shall receive compensation in the way of reserves of land, payments, annuities and presents, in manner similar to that set forth in the several respects for the Indians in the said treaty; it being understood, however, that any sum expended annually by Her Majesty in the purchase of

This is the rough diagram alluded to in the agreement to which
the same is attached shewing the Reserves for the Half-
breeds on the westerly shore of the Rainy Lake

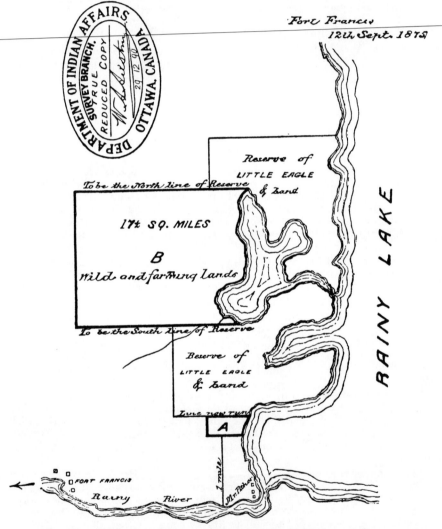

A. *To be 160 acres for Halfbreeds to build and live on as a*
village

B *To extend from south to North limit of large Bay as shewn*
and to extend westerly to embrace 17½ square miles

(sgd) **J.S.D.**
N. C.

ammunition and twine for nets for the use of the said Half-breeds shall not be taken out of the fifteen hundred dollars set apart by the treaty for the purchase annually of those articles for the Indians, but shall be in addition thereto, and shall be a *pro rata* amount in the proportion of the number of Half-breeds parties hereto to the number of Indians embraced in the treaty; and it being further understood that the said Half-breeds shall be entitled to all the benefits of the said treaty as from the date thereof, as regards payments and annuities, in the same manner as if they had been present and had become parties to the same at the time of the making thereof.

And whereas the said Half-breeds desire the land set forth as tracts marked (A) and (B) on the rough diagram attached hereto, and marked with the initials of the parties aforementioned to this agreement, as their reserves (in all eighteen square miles), to which they would be entitled under the provisions of the treaty, the same is hereby agreed to on the part of the Government.

Should this agreement be approved by the Government, the reserves as above to be surveyed in due course.

Signed at Fort Francis, the day and date above mentioned, in presence of us as witnesses:
    A. R. TILLIE,
    CHAS. S. CROWE,
    W. B. RICHARDSON,
    L. KITTSON.

J. S. DENNIS,   [L.S.]
    his
NICHOLAS x CHATELAINE.   [L.S.]
    mark.

ADHESION OF LAC SEUL INDIANS TO TREATY No. 3

LAC SEUL, 9th June, 1874.

We, the Chiefs and Councillors of Lac Seul, Seul, Trout and Sturgeon Lakes, subscribe and set our marks, that we and our followers will abide by the articles of the Treaty made and concluded with the Indians at the North West Angle of the Lake of the Woods, on the third day of October, in the year of Our Lord one thousand eight hundred and seventy-three, between Her Most Gracious Majesty the Queen of Great Britain and Ireland, by Her Commissioners, Hon. Alexander Morris, Lieutenant Governor of Manitoba and the North-West Territories, Joseph Albert N. Provencher, and Simon J. Dawson, of the one part, and the Saulteaux tribes of Ojibewas Indians, inhabitants of the country as defined by the Treaty aforesaid.

IN WITNESS WHEREOF, Her Majesty's Indian Agent and the Chiefs and Councillors have hereto set their hands at Lac Seul, on the 9th day of June, 1874.

(Signed)   R. J. N. PITHER, *Indian Agent.*
    JOHN CROMARTY, his x mark,
        Chief.
    ACKEMENCE, his x mark.
    MAINEETAINEQUIRE, his x mark.
    NAH-KEE-JECKWAHE, his x mark,
        Councillors.

The whole Treaty explained by R. J. N. PITHER.

Witnesses:
    (Signed)   JAMES MCKENZIE.
        LOUIS KITTSON.
           his
        NICHOLAS x CHATELAINE.
           mark.

WOODLAND PERIOD

ARCHAIC PERIOD

Sioux
Assiniboines
Monsonis
Cree
Ojibway →

BLACK DUCK CULTURE

LAUREL CULTURE

Rock Paintings

Dead Buried in Pits
and Covered with Small
Mounds

Bow and Arrow
Huge Burial Mounds
Pottery

Use of Copper tools
and weapons

Use of Stone, Wood, Antlers,
Bone and ivory for weapons
and tools

1700

1500 AD

1000 AD

500 AD

Birth of Christ

500 BC

1000 BC

1500 BC

2000 BC

La Vérendrye and Fort St.
Charles (1732)

DeNoyon discovers Lake of
the Woods (1688)

Approximate present shoreline
of Lake of the Woods established

Lake of the Woods as part of
Lake Agassiz

Time Line #1

Prehistoric to the coming of the white man.

1975

1950

1925

Fort St. Charles site discovered (1908)

1900 Railroad comes to south end of Lake of the Woods (1890)
Gold rush begins
Massacre Island identified (1890)

1875 Coming of the railroad to Kenora (1881)   John Mather

Indian Treaty #3 (1873)
George Dawson seeks all-Canadian route west (1873)
1850 Wolseley Expedition (1870)
Simon Dawson seeks all-Canadian route to Winnipeg area (1857)
Rat Portage Trading Post established (1836)

1825

American Fur Trading Company comes to Lake of the Woods (1821); Merger of Hudson's Bay Co. and North West Trading Co. (1821)

1800

John Tanner - defender of Indians and other trappers against North West Trading Company; Treaty of Paris (1783) - France gives up rights to Canadian North America to England; North
1775 West Angle first drawn.

1750
The Massacre (1736)
The La Verendryes come to Lake of the Woods and build Fort St. Charles (1732)

1725
Pachot charts Pigeon River and follows southernly route to Lake (1722); De la Noue builds trading post at mouth of Kaministiquia River and comes to Rainy Lake area (1717)

1700

Jacques de Noyon discovers Lake of the Woods (1688)

1675

Chartering of Hudson Bay Company (1670)

1650

1625

Time Line #2

From the Age of Discovery and Exploration to the Present.

Gold Mining

Logging and Lumbering

Tourism

Commercial Fishing

Steamboat era

Voyageurs

Age of Exploration